TIME

Paul McCartney

The Legend Rocks On

BY JAMES KAPLAN

TIME

MANAGING EDITOR Richard Stengel
DESIGN DIRECTOR D.W. Pine
DIRECTOR OF PHOTOGRAPHY Kira Pollack

Paul McCartney

The Legend Rocks On

EDITOR Stephen Koepp
WRITER James Kaplan
DESIGNER Arthur Hochstein
PHOTO EDITOR Patricia Cadley
RESEARCHERS Elizabeth L. Bland, Molly Martin
COPY EDITOR Barbara Collier
EDITORIAL PRODUCTION Lionel P. Vargas

TIME HOME ENTERTAINMENT

PUBLISHER Richard Fraiman
VICE PRESIDENT, BUSINESS DEVELOPMENT AND STRATEGY Steven Sandonato
EXECUTIVE DIRECTOR, MARKETING SERVICES Carol Pittard
EXECUTIVE DIRECTOR, RETAIL AND SPECIAL SALES Tom Mifsud
EXECUTIVE PUBLISHING DIRECTOR Joy Butts
DIRECTOR, BOOKAZINE DEVELOPMENT AND MARKETING Laura Adam
FINANCE DIRECTOR Glenn Buonocore
ASSISTANT GENERAL COUNSEL Helen Wan
ASSISTANT DIRECTOR, SPECIAL SALES Ilene Schreider
BOOK PRODUCTION MANAGER Suzanne Janso
DESIGN AND PREPRESS MANAGER Anne-Michelle Gallero
BRAND MANAGER Michela Wilde
ASSOCIATE BRAND MANAGER Isata Yansaneh

SPECIAL THANKS TO:
Christine Austin, Katherine Barnet, Jeremy Biloon, Stephanie Braga, Jim Childs, Susan Chodakiewicz, Rose Cirrincione, Lauren Hall Clark, Jacqueline Fitzgerald, Christine Font, Jenna Goldberg, Hillary Hirsch, Amy Mangus, Robert Marasco, Kimberly Marshall, Amy Migliaccio, Nina Mistry, Dave Rozzelle, Adriana Tierno, Vanessa Wu, TIME Imaging

ISBN 10: 1-61893-024-9
ISBN 13: 978-1-61893-024-8
Library of Congress Control Number: 2012931014

We welcome your comments and suggestions about TIME Books. Please write to us at:
TIME Books, Attention: Book Editors, P.O. Box 11016, Des Moines, IA 50336-1016

If you would like to order any of our hardcover Collector's Edition books, please call us at 1-800-327-6388, Monday through Friday, 7 a.m. to 8 p.m., or Saturday, 7 a.m. to 6 p.m., Central Time.

Contents

ABOUT THE AUTHOR James Kaplan, a novelist, journalist and biographer, has written seven books, including his best-selling 2010 life of Frank Sinatra, *Frank: The Voice.* He is the recipient of a 2012 Guggenheim Fellowship.

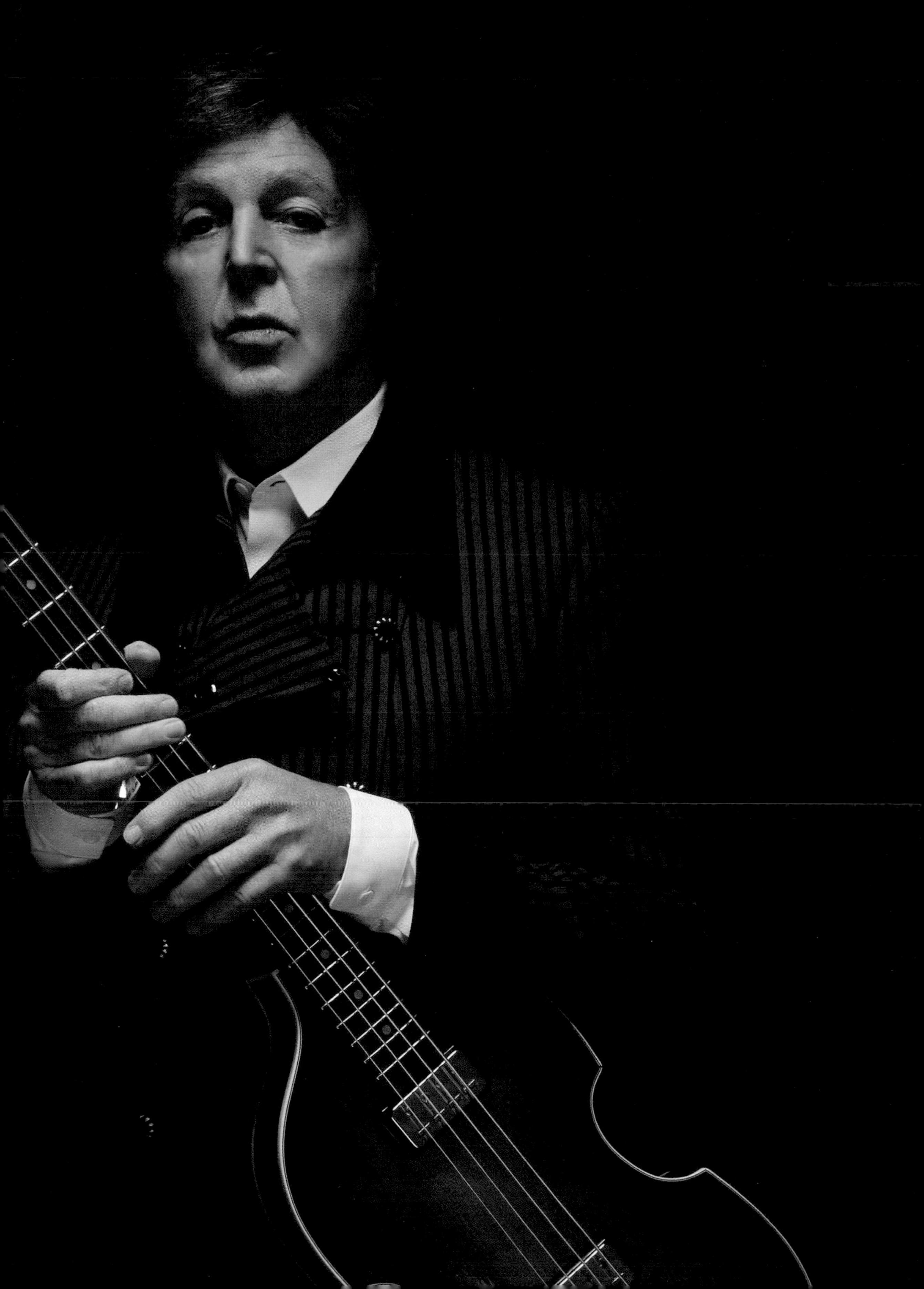

Love Me Do

The extraordinary life of an ordinary man—
Paul McCartney, at 70, still rocks our world

Beatlemania erupts as the band plays its first concert in the U.S., on Feb. 11, 1964, at the Washington Coliseum. Two days earlier, the Beatles had appeared on *The Ed Sullivan Show*.

In 1970, with the Beatles disbanded and his solo career under way, Paul elevates his wife Linda to singing partner, and they record the *Ram* album in New York City.

Onstage in Buenos Aires in 2010, Paul enjoys the show as much as his fans do. He had always been the Beatle who most relished live performing, and he maintains a grueling global touring schedule even in his seventh decade.

H

E IS THE MOST ORDINARY OF extraordinary men: a historical figure with a common streak, a genius who's still not entirely sure where it all comes from, or came from.

"I've always had this thing of him and me," Paul McCartney told Barry Miles, his authorized biographer, in 1996. "He goes onstage, he's famous, and then me; I'm just some kid from Liverpool ... this little kid who used to run down the streets in Speke ... collecting jam jars, damming up streams in the woods. I still very much am him grown up.

"Occasionally, I stop and think, I am Paul McCartney ... hell, that is a total freak-out! You know, Paul McCartney! Just the words, it sounds like a total kind of legend. But, of course, you don't want to go thinking that too much because it takes over." And yet, "when I go on tour, I'm glad of the legendary thing," he said. "I wouldn't want to try and entertain 60,000 people in a Texas stadium with just the guy next door."

No, that wouldn't do at all. And so—still, in 2012—he steps out on the stage of whatever arena he may be playing, in whichever corner of the world—it scarcely matters where or what language they speak; everyone knows him and loves him, everyone knows the words to all the songs—and, as the roar rises to the rafters, begins singing, for the umpteenth time and with undiminished joy:

Roll up, roll up for the magical mystery tour, step right this way ...

ON JUNE 18—INCONCEIVABLY—he turns 70, and he's still rolling. Fast. In the months before the big day, he seemed to be everywhere at once: touring in Helsinki and Moscow and Liverpool. Getting a star on the Hollywood Walk of Fame. Playing at the MusiCares benefit (where he was honored as Person of the Year). Playing at the Grammys. Attending his daughter Stella's fashion show in Paris. Vacationing in St. Barts with his wife Nancy Shevell—and then touring some more, in Rotterdam and Zurich and London.

It was almost as though, if he moved fast enough and squeezed in enough events, he might sideslip the 18th of June altogether and proceed to the next golden stage, untouched and untallied. Exactly the kind of dream a little kid running down the street in Liverpool might dream.

Except that no one, in his wildest imaginings, could have dreamed all that had happened to him in the years between then and now.

All four of them had remarkable faces, but only his was beautiful, the big-eyed, long-lashed looks saved from mere prettiness by a persistent, perhaps willfully untended, five-o'clock shadow and those asymmetrical, ironically arched brows, which seemed to say, *I've got the goods. No, really. Think I'm kidding?*

He had the goods, and then some. "Oh, beyond measure—on a Mozart level," the musician and record producer Peter Asher told TIME recently, speaking of the musical gifts of the brash young Liverpudlian who, beginning in 1963, dated his sister Jane and, though already famous, bunked in the attic of the Asher family's town house on Wimpole Street: the attic where the melody of "Yesterday" came to him one night in a dream.

That, of course, was many yesterdays ago. And while Paul McCartney's youthful beauty has gone the way of youth, the immense musical talent endures, along with, at the biblical three score and 10, something perhaps even more remarkable: "He keeps on going," says another longtime acquaintance, the writer and director Michael Lindsay-Hogg. "He doesn't have to. He's got all the money and all the success, and he's written some great songs. In Tennessee Williams' *Camino Real* ... there's [a line]: 'Make voyages, attempt them; there's nothing else.' I think that's Paul."

At 70, he voyages still, maintaining a schedule that would give pause to a man half his age: a 30-concert tour in 2011-2012, from the Bronx to Bologna, Moscow to Montevideo to Mexico City. "My wife says he's an alien from the Planet Fab," says Paul "Wix" Wickens, the keyboardist in the band that has backed McCartney for the past 10 years. (The band also includes bassist Rusty Anderson, guitarist/bassist Brian Ray and drummer Abe Laboriel Jr.)

"If you're enjoying it, why do something else?" McCartney asked *Rolling Stone,* rhetorically, earlier this year. His pleasure in his art and his craft seems as pure as it was when he first picked up a guitar almost 60 years ago. "He absolutely loves music," Wickens says. "He loves to play. And he loves being involved. He's always doing something. When we [in the band] are not working, he is not not-working. He does relax, and he does take holidays. But he puts his head into other places, not just pop music, because he likes a challenge, he likes just to be doing it."

Last fall the New York City Ballet premiered McCartney's fifth classical work, *Ocean's Kingdom* ("[I]n no way an important addition to the corpus of ballet music, but ... it has plenty of color and melody," said the New York *Times*); this February he released a well-received CD of American Songbook standards, *Kisses on the Bottom.* Under the pseudonym "The Fireman," he has made three albums of ambient electronic music.

But love remains his great subject. Though *Ocean's Kingdom* is cloaked in a cautionary ecological message—the undersea good guys are threatened by terrestrial baddies—it's still the story of a couple trying to make it against the world's intrusions. McCartney knows what that feels like. His first two marriages were largely conducted in the spotlight's glare: his late first wife, Linda Eastman McCartney, performed with him for over 25 years, both as part of Wings and afterward; he and his second wife, Heather Mills, were tabloid fodder during their brief and turbulent union and their highly public divorce.

Now, on the strength of his third marriage, Paul McCartney seems to be trying to get the him-and-me thing right at last. Fifty-one-year-old Nancy Shevell is that rarest of all birds in Paul's life, an intensely private figure. Unlike his first two wives, she is neither blond nor buxom; unlike Linda and Heather, who were outspoken about their causes (vegetarianism, in Linda's case; land mines and amputees, in Heather's), the slim, dark-haired Shevell—a survivor of breast cancer, the disease that killed Paul's mother and first wife—doesn't speak for the public record.

Paul is the one who does that—though master politician that he is, he keeps the message as upbeat and general as possible. "[T]o find love after a divorce is great—it's very refreshing," he told *Rolling Stone.* "And Nancy's great: she's intriguing, interesting, lovely, smart, emotional and all the things you would want in a mate. She's absolutely beautiful. She's funny, she's canny, she's great—it's all there."

That's three *greats,* if you were counting.

Good thing he lets his lyrics do the talking. "What if it rained?/ We didn't care," he wrote in "My Valentine," a dark and tender song he composed for her not long after they met. The couple had traveled to Morocco together; the weather had been wet instead of fine; afterward, Paul said, Shevell had spoken those words to him. They were the words of a couple taking shelter together against a world that has intruded too often and too much.

And—tellingly—it's a love song in a minor key, written by a man famed for writing in sunny tones: a tacit acknowledgment of the shadow of loss that has fallen across much of McCartney's life, an admission that all our arrangements are ultimately temporary.

Shevell, an executive in her family's trucking company and wealthy in her own right, "came in self-contained," says Wickens. "She is always written up in the papers as 'Nancy Shevell, the socialite,' though she is a working woman in a tough world. She still goes back to work. But I think because she came in self-contained, it was easier for them to have a balanced relationship. Marriage in the end is teamwork as much as anything else, and you have to make a good team to have some kind of chance of surviving. I think that's what's happened there. [It's] kind of what you have to do in any relationship ultimately, once you've got past the hearts and flowers."

PURE EMOTION, THOUGH, is the through-line of every concert McCartney plays these days. For nearly three hours, over the course of some 35 songs—roughly half of them Beatles numbers—he runs the gamut of feeling from the quiet pensiveness of "Yesterday" to the throat-tearing swagger of "Helter Skelter"; from the joy of "Jet," "All My Loving" and "Back in the U.S.S.R." to the soulfulness of "The Long and Winding Road," "Maybe I'm Amazed" and, of course, "Hey Jude," the anthem John Lennon always felt Paul had written to and about him.

The spirit of his acerbic ex-partner, the man who lent the grit to their greatness, is present, explicitly or implicitly, in every McCartney show. He often performs mini-medleys of the Lennon numbers "A Day in the Life"/"Give Peace a Chance" and "The Word"/"All You Need Is Love"; and smack in the middle of every set, the band leaves the stage while he sits with an acoustic guitar and, after performing "Blackbird," sings his tribute to John, "Here Today." "On the 21st time he sings it, he'll [still] choke up because he's inhabiting the songs as he sings them," Wickens says. "He'll start to well up and have to gather himself. Because he's living in the songs. That's what you get when you come to the show. That's why they work."

For a long time after his first band broke up, McCartney would cut people off if they asked him about those days: the wounds were still too raw. Then, as the years passed, he softened: the number of Beatles numbers he performed in each show slowly increased. These days he seems unapologetically nostalgic: not living in the past but cherishing it. "I've noticed the older he gets, the more he loves to think about the Beatles," Paul's cousin Kate Robbins tells me. "He's always great with the stories."

On the other hand, Wickens says, "About the legacy, I'm not sure he gets that—how big it is and what it means to other people. He loves the songs. He loves to play them. We see what a big deal it is to people because you see three generations at the shows, and at certain points, they fall apart if it's a particularly meaningful song. It goes very deep with people."

Everywhere. In Northern Europe and Japan, the audiences sit and listen politely, almost worshipfully. "They are attentive. They clap in between. Then when you go off the stage, they go bananas," Wickens says. "Whereas South American audiences and the more Latin audiences are very loud and noisy, sing-along. In Mexico, they just go bananas all the way through, singing and shouting, having a party. They sing so loud in the stadium that it's hard when you do 'Yesterday' sometimes to hear above your own monitors. They sing everything. They even do the guitar bit to 'Day Tripper.'"

And what about when McCartney plays his hometown? "Liverpudlians have a particular sense of humor," Wickens tells me. "So they will hold him dear but rib him mercilessly. We played at one gig there where one of them yelled from the back, 'Hey, Paul, buy us a house!'"

It's exactly the kind of joke the world's most famous Liverpudlian might make himself. Witness a similar story told by his cousin Kate Robbins: "We have a cousin's husband called Ronnie Fogg who is famous in the family because he's just so irreverent with Paul. All he ever says [is], 'Hey, Paul—buy us a pub. Hey, Paul—give us a million.' And Paul says, 'Hey, Ronnie—you don't need a pub. All you need is *luhhv*.'"

Funny, the things an ordinary man will come up with.

At 69, McCartney gets married, for the third time, to Nancy Shevell, 51, at the same London town hall where he was first wed.

Paul's Top

1. I Saw Her Standing There After the "one-two-three-*faw*" intro, the hand claps, the ooohs and the song's unleashed energy explode like a teenage rock-'n'-roll cluster bomb. You know what I mean.

2. Hey Jude A paean to Julian Lennon, although John thought it was for him. Figures. No matter, melodically and vocally, it's Paul's masterpiece—and at seven minutes, 11 seconds, one of the longest singles in history.

3. Let It Be "It's a love song." "It's a spiritual." Stop! You're both right. Written around one of his mother's aphorisms, it is as much a standard as "Amazing Grace" or "As Time Goes By," and as identifiable as "Chopsticks."

4. Here, There, and Everywhere Written for girlfriend Jane Asher and influenced by the sophistication of *Pet Sounds,* it frames a seductive melody with heartfelt romance. John called it "one of my favorite songs of the Beatles."

5. Yesterday One of the most covered songs in history. Originally called "Scrambled Eggs," it was an instant classic. Daffy Duck's version will make you cry.

6. Eleanor Rigby Why would anybody keep a face in a jar by the door? The song is too poignant, lush and musically gorgeous to ponder such riddles. Perhaps Paul's most cinematic lyric, as filmed by Fellini.

7. The Fool on the Hill Another fine-toned, if desolate, beauty, crafted with assurance and restraint. John cited it as proof that Paul could write a killer lyric, "if he's a good boy."

8. For No One One of Paul's quietest beauties accompanied by a haunting French-horn solo that underscores the song's melancholy, written after an argument with Jane Asher.

9. She Loves You "Yeah-yeah-yeah." That's all you need to know.

10. All My Loving Every teenage girl heard this sung directly to her—and when Paul batted those doe eyes, it sealed the deal.

TIME asked Bob Spitz, author of the best-selling The Beatles: The Biography, *to rank the songs primarily written by Paul. Spitz's next book,* Dearie: The Remarkable Life of Julia Child, *is to be published in August 2012.*

11. Got to Get You Into My Life Paul takes all the R&B material from early Beatles shows and stuffs it into one feverish rocker. Those stinging horns are almost as super-charged as his vocal. "One of his best songs," according to John.

12. And I Love Her Could anyone make such a saccharine statement sound more convincing? It's about as polished—and haunting—a love song as any adolescent could muster.

13. Penny Lane A rock song so technically skillful and structurally crafted, it might have been designed by Frank Lloyd Wright. Paul's wistful ode to an old neighborhood haunt.

14. Can't Buy Me Love Paul finally perfected the pop hit with this frisky single from *A Hard Day's Night,* which catapulted to the top of the charts faster than any previous song.

15. The Long and Winding Road Written just before the Beatles split. Musically, it's over the top—and then some. But Paul sells schmaltz better than a Jewish butcher.

16. We Can Work It Out Another heartfelt ballad written in the aftermath of an argument with Jane Asher. Why he ever stopped fighting with her we'll never understand.

17. Maybe I'm Amazed A musical tour de force on which Paul played every instrument himself, and the vocal is spine tingling. His first single after the band split—Beatles fans never forgave him.

18. Eight Days a Week The working title for *Help!* Paul cadged the phrase from one of Ringo's wacky sayings. The harmonies with John, powered by hand claps, fill the tank with excitement.

19. Blackbird Paul's attempt to write about the civil rights struggle. Really. The elegant guitar line is based on Bach's "Bourrée in E-minor." Really.

20. Get Back Originally written as a satire skewing the anti-immigrant sentiment in the U.K., it got upstaged by Sweet Loretta Martin and 20 megatons of funk. John naturally heard it as a knock on Yoko.

40

Beatles Expert Bob Spitz Spent A Hard Day's Night Choosing The Best McCartney Songs

21. **Michelle** You can hear him trying so hard to write the Great Pop Standard, and in a sense, he did. But it might have been better served by Englebert Humperdinck, *n'est-ce pas?*

22. **Jet** Just when it seemed as though Paul had lost his way came this killer track from *Band on the Run,* a turbocharged rocker that threw his pipes back into overdrive.

23. **Things We Said Today** Written during a Caribbean vacation with Jane Asher, it's rather bittersweet for a love song, but its gentle simplicity shines through.

24. **She's Leaving Home** Inspired by a news item about a teenage runaway, Paul dramatized it from the parents' perspective. Brian Wilson reportedly cried when Paul played it for him.

25. **I've Just Seen a Face** Paul loved the way the lyric kept dragging the listener to the next line of this two-minute song—but blink and you've missed it.

26. **Yellow Submarine** If you have kids, you're ready to scratch the grooves off the record. But it's iconic—the ultimate kiddie-pleaser—and only Ringo could have sold it that well. Donovan helped with the lyrics.

27. **Band on the Run** The hit that most separates him from the Beatles' legacy: a remarkable ensemble groove, with stylish musical turns, that emphasizes his evident command.

28. **Every Night** A hidden gem from his first solo album, written for Linda with such aching tenderness.

29. **Drive My Car** As close to all-out rock 'n' roll as the mid-career Beatles ever got. The song was edited out of *Rubber Soul* in favor of folkier numbers. "Beep-beep and beep-beep, yeah!"

30. **Back in the U.S.S.R.** A propulsive kick-off to the *White Album*—part Chuck Berry, part Beach Boys and a hundred percent Beatlesque. When Paul criticized the drumming on it, Ringo temporarily quit the band, forcing McCartney to whip off the backbeat with inimitable skill.

31. **With a Little Help From My Friends** The song that launched a thousand commercials, but a *Sgt. Pepper's* standout. Cut during an all-night session, after the grueling photo shoot for that unforgettable album cover.

32. **My Love** Sappy, absolutely—but so lush and plaintive. The song builds to its Mantovani climax with dramatic fluency. Wedding planners rejoiced.

33. **Paperback Writer** Even though the Beatles had created the genre of artful rock, they could still kick out the jams. John called this single "the son of 'Day Tripper'"—a rock-'n'-roll song with a guitar lick on a fuzzy loud guitar."

34. **Lady Madonna** His ode to the Irish working-class woman. Not much of a penetrating song, but, oh, what a piano lick! Paul claimed alternately that it was lifted from either Fats Domino or Humphrey Littleton's "Bad Penny Blues."

35. **Hello Goodbye** The ultimate iPhone ringtone. Another cleverly crafted Beatles throwaway single that served the whimsical character of its flip-side, "I Am the Walrus," perfectly.

36. **Ob-La-Di, Ob-La-Da** Written on excursions with the Maharishi to the open-air markets in Rishikesh, India. The title was a Yoruba phrase he'd picked up from Jimmy Scott, a conga player from the London club scene.

37. **She Came in Through the Bathroom Window** Written when he first met Linda, it was part of the *Abbey Road* medley that resonates well beyond its fragmented parts. The deceptive bridge—"Didn't anybody tell her?"—is another tribute to Paul's musical virtuosity.

38. **Live and Let Die** O.K., it's no "Goldfinger," not even a "Nobody Does It Better," but as James Bond themes go, just try getting it out of your head.

39. **P.S. I Love You** Written when the Beatles were evolving, in Hamburg. According to John, "he was trying to write a 'Soldier Boy,' like the Shirelles."

40. **I'm Looking Through You** Apparently an autobiographical song chronicling the end of his relationship with Jane Asher, after the Beatles returned from an American tour. Its elegiac quality underscores the song's deeply felt sincerity.

CHAPTER 1

Paul's first instrument is the trumpet, but not long after his 14th birthday, he trades it in for a guitar.

A Match Made

AN INCISED SANDSTONE PLAQUE ON THE

wall of St. Peter's Church Hall in Woolton, a sleepy suburb on the outskirts of Liverpool, commemorates the event as if it had religious significance—as indeed it very nearly does:

IN THIS HALL ON
6TH JULY 1957
JOHN & PAUL
FIRST MET

No need to ask about last names.

The afternoon was oppressively hot and humid. The occasion was a church fete, a few

John leads his band, the Quarrymen, at a church fete on July 6, 1957, the day he meets 15-year-old Paul, who dazzles with songs by Eddie Cochran and Little Richard.

in Liverpool

summer hours of festivities in the yard next to St. Peter's cemetery: lemonade and ice cream and cakes and musical acts and performing horses and police dogs. Lots of kids. One of the acts was a group of local boys called the Quarrymen, named after the public high school they attended, Quarry Bank (itself named after Woolton Quarry, where sandstone was mined). The band played skiffle—kind of an English variety of jug-band music popular in the '50s, thumped out on guitar, banjo, drums and tea-chest bass—along with a little rock 'n' roll. Its singer and lead guitarist, a sideburned, eagle-nosed 16-year-old in a checked cowboy shirt with the collar turned up, preferred rock 'n' roll. John Lennon could barely play his guitar—it had only four strings, and he used banjo chords—but with his hoarse yet tuneful voice and cheeky attitude, he was spellbinding. Among the band's rock repertory was the Del-Vikings' "Come Go with Me." Lennon, not really knowing the words, simply made up his own: "Come go with me/ Down to the penitentiary …" Somehow he made it work.

By November 1957, Paul is in the Quarrymen, and Elvis' "Heartbreak Hotel," released a year earlier, is drawing the band toward rock 'n' roll.

After the fete, there was to be a grand dance in the Village Hall across the road. George Edge's Orchestra would play for the adults; the Quarrymen would entertain the kids. As the long summer twilight faded, thunder rumbled portentously; the heat wave would break that night. As the skiffle group took its instruments into the hall, a close friend of Lennon's named Ivan Vaughan approached him with a request: Did he have any interest in meeting another friend of his, a boy who could sing and play guitar? The boy was good, Vaughan said.

In a few minutes, Lennon found out how good. The boy, a cherub-faced 15-year-old with big hazel eyes, pouty lips and his dark hair slicked back rock-'n'-roll style, was ceremoniously dressed in a white sports jacket backed with silver threads: a showy touch that Lennon, in his tight teddy-boy jeans and cowboy shirt, would have found disconcerting.

Then Paul McCartney asked to borrow a guitar.

The Quarrymen's instruments were strung for right-handers; McCartney was a lefty. No matter. He'd dealt with this problem before: you simply played upside-down. And that's what he did, performing a near letter-perfect cover of Eddie Cochran's fast-moving mouthful "Twenty

Flight Rock," to the astonishment of Lennon and his bandmates. "I knew a lot of the words," McCartney later recalled. "That was very good currency in those days."

Then the young natural showman decided to top that.

McCartney sat down at the hall's upright piano and blazed through Little Richard's "Long Tall Sally." "It was uncanny," Quarrymen guitarist Eric Griffiths told Bob Spitz, author of *The Beatles,* many years later. "He could play and sing in a way that none of us could, including John. He had such confidence; he gave a *performance*. It was so natural. We couldn't get enough of it. It was a real eye opener."

For his part, Lennon recalled (to Beatles biographer Hunter Davies), "I half thought to myself, 'He's as good as me.' Now I thought, if I take him on, what will happen? It went through my head that I'd have to keep him in line if I let him join [the band]. But he was good, so he was worth having. He also looked like Elvis. I dug him."

That was an understatement. From that day forward, the two would be inextricably bound, in each other's minds as well as the world's.

The McCartneys: from left, Paul's little brother Mike, Mary, Jim and Paul. Mary would die of cancer at age 47, about nine months before Paul met John.

Liverpool in the 1950s, a grimy, red brick port city, is peculiarly receptive to American rock 'n' roll. Soon it becomes an export.

THE DOE-EYED PHENOM WHO rocked John Lennon's world that hot July afternoon was, underneath the white sports jacket and the bravado, far more vulnerable than he let on. Paul McCartney's adored mother, Mary, a midwife and visiting nurse, had died of breast cancer, at age 47, only nine months earlier, leaving Paul, his younger brother, Mike, and their father, Jim, an amateur musician who worked as a salesman for a Liverpool cotton firm, to try to muddle through without her.

For several months, they barely made it: Jim was reeling with grief. "That was the worst thing for me, hearing my dad cry," Paul remembered. "You expect to see women crying or kids in the playground or even yourself … But when it's your dad, then you know something's really wrong, and it shakes your faith in everything. But I was determined not to let it affect me. I carried on. I learned to put a shell around me at that age."

Music was the main component of the shell. It came naturally: the whole extended McCartney family was musical. As a young man in the 1920s, Jim had fronted a dance band, and he still played a mean piano by ear ("His left one," Paul McCartney liked to joke).

The McCartneys made music whenever they got together, and at first, trumpet was Paul's instrument. But he was also beginning to listen to American rock 'n' roll late at night on Radio Luxembourg—there was no rock on English radio in those days—and to grow intoxicated by its rhythms. Rock 'n' roll wasn't about trumpets. And then there was the fact that you couldn't sing while you played a horn.

Rock was hitting England like a slow-moving tsunami in the mid-'50s. Prior to 1950, as Liverpool local historian Joan Murray explains, "there were no teenagers." Especially in that rough-

**The McCartney family home on Forthlin Road
is a council flat, cramped in size, built by the
government to improve housing after World War II.**

hewn, northern port city along the River Mersey, where working-class and middle-class kids mostly just got out of school and got on with life. But Liverpool, so red brick dingy and looked down upon by London, was also peculiarly receptive to rock 'n' roll—in part, because of the steady inflow of American culture through the docks. Now, suddenly, amid the postwar recovery, Liverpool kids had a couple of shillings to rub together, and with the records they were buying—records by Little Richard, Chuck Berry, Buddy Holly and, especially, Elvis—came new dreams.

Shortly after his 14th birthday, Paul went to a downtown music shop and traded his trumpet for a Zenith acoustic guitar. He practiced obsessively, struggling to teach himself chords, but everything felt backward to the left-hander, until he hit on the idea of restringing the instrument—with the bass and treble strings reversed.

In the wake of his mother's death, his obsession with the instrument redoubled. He would lock himself in the bathroom and practice for hours at a time. Initially a promising student—English literature and languages (Spanish and German) were his best subjects—at the prestigious public Liverpool Institute, he began to neglect his studies for the one thing that could take him away from all his troubles. When John Lennon sent a message (through a bandmate named Pete Shotton) asking him to join the Quarrymen, Paul McCartney didn't have to think twice.

Skiffle stayed in the group's repertoire for a while, but Lennon had little patience for it. Elvis Presley's "Heartbreak Hotel" had electrified him (as it had McCartney). That—the sound, the look, the attitude—was what he was after. Meanwhile, the band started to break apart, as Lennon and his original mates graduated from Quarry Bank in 1958, and all but John, the dreamer and misfit, drifted off toward real life. But McCartney had introduced Lennon to a younger schoolmate from the Institute, a tiny, cocky 14-year-old, with jug ears and big hair. His name was George Harrison. "George was my little friend," McCartney recalled many years later, with fond condescension. "But he could play guitar." And George liked rock 'n' roll.

McCartney helped Lennon advance on the instrument, and with the big-eared little guy playing lead, all at once they were a rock-'n'-roll trio. On Sept. 18, 1959, a front-page story in the *West Derby Reporter* covered the recent opening of the Casbah, a new club for teenagers in the Liverpool suburb. The club was in the windowless basement of a huge, rambling old house in a residential neighborhood—the performance space, such as it was, the size of a coal bin. The account went on to mention "a guitar group which entertains the club members on Saturday nights … [T]he group, who call themselves 'The Quarrymen,' travel from the south end of the city to play. They are: John Lennon, Menlove Avenue, Woolton; Paul McCartney, Forthlin Road, Allerton; and George Harrison, Upton Green, Speke."

A photo with the story shows McCartney, soulful in dark shirt and light tie, confidently

George Harrison, 12, works on his licks. He has two more years of practice before joining the band.

In September 1959, still known as the Quarrymen, the band starts making local headlines when it appears on Saturday nights at a new teen club in a Liverpool basement called the Casbah.

strumming his guitar and singing into a mike while Lennon, seemingly a little less sure of his playing, stares down at his instrument, carefully fingering a chord. Two girls and a boy sit on a bench to the right, paying careful attention. The caption reads: "Three 'cool cats' listen to 'The Quarrymen.'" The polite-looking, well-dressed young English people resemble anything but cool cats. The girl on the left, smiling at McCartney, is Cynthia Powell, who will later marry Lennon.

OR MAYBE LENNON'S downward stare is brooding. One evening the previous summer, John's spirited and flighty mother, Julia, who consigned him at age 5 to the care of her tightly wound, ultra-responsible eldest sister, Mary Elizabeth—Mimi—had been hit by a car and killed, after paying John and Mimi a visit.

"That was our biggest bond—our mums had died when we were teenaged," McCartney said, years later. There were all kinds of bonds, rock 'n' roll not the least of them. Yet the connection of sorrow, not spoken about but felt, was the deepest. It guaranteed mutual trust; it fenced out other, less-suffering souls.

But music ran a close second. The two boys, each a kind of genius, perhaps not quite

Working partners: The songwriting team emerges, as Paul and John, in the living room of Paul's Liverpool house, polish a tune that will become "I Saw Her Standing There."

knowing it yet but sensing an inner difference from other people, were, without exaggeration, thrilled by each other—exhilarated to find, in this bleak northern landscape of commerce and conformity, a kindred, wild spirit.

A pair of photographs taken a couple of years later by Mike McCartney tells the whole story: Paul and John sit with their guitars in the tiny living room at 20 Forthlin Road, writing the song that will become "I Saw Her Standing There." A school notebook with handwritten lyrics sits on the floor at Paul's feet. With their instruments facing opposite ways, the two young men are able to sit nearly elbow to elbow—just a hair's breadth separates them—and the powerful bond between them is instantly apparent. "I think it was Cynthia Lennon who said, 'John and Paul were as different as chalk and cheese individually, but joined at the hip musically,'" says Colin Hall of the National Trust, who's showing me around McCartney's boyhood home. I stare at the photos. Besides the physical closeness, there's the look on both their faces, respectful and attentive. And then this small but telling detail: John is wearing his black-rimmed eyeglasses, without which he is "blind as a bat," according to Paul, but which his vanity keeps him from wearing most places, especially in public. But this isn't public; it's very private. The intimacy is startling.

At the same time, the two were rivals from the beginning, in songwriting and for control of the band. Lennon sensed it the instant he heard McCartney play: *If I take him on, what will happen?* They took each other on, really—in both senses of the loaded phrase, becoming competitors as well as friends and collaborators, inspiring and irritating and goading the best from each other. "They were so close, so very close, and competitive," Bill Harry, a classmate of John's at Liverpool College of Art and the founder of *Mersey Beat Magazine,* which covered the city's exploding rock scene in the early '60s, told TIME. "But it was good competitiveness. 'I'm going to beat you, but I'm not going to beat you as an enemy. We're in the competition together. I'll win one day, and you'll win the other day.'"

And then there was this: they were virtually from opposite sides of the tracks. "John lived in the posh part of Liverpool," Harry says. "A garden front and back, indoor bathroom, indoor toilet, all that. Most of us—no bathroom, outdoor toilets, all the rest of it." This was how Ringo Starr and George Harrison grew up. And while the McCartneys' Forthlin Road house had both a bathroom and an indoor toilet, it was a council flat, built by the government to try to improve housing stock after the war, and had the tight interior dimensions and generic feeling of government housing.

Aunt Mimi's place on Menlove Avenue was a different matter altogether. Though the house, called Mendips (the original builders in the 1930s had named the home, as a tony touch,

after a picturesque range of hills in southwest England), was semi-detached rather than freestanding, and though Mimi couldn't quite afford it (she had to take in boarders), it, like its owner, had airs. With its half-timbered Tudor interior and tulip-inlaid, leaded-glass windows, its airy kitchen and elegant front sitting room and spacious backyard, it was every inch the bourgeois showplace, and the working-class boy from Forthlin Road was duly awed by it, if not cowed. "I was kind of seeing another world from what I was used to," Paul recalled. "I remember being very impressed in Mendips with the entire works of Winston Churchill. And John had read 'em! I hadn't met people like this ...

"I remember Mimi saying [to John], 'Your little friend's here to see you.' That kind of thing, where you know she's belittling you—then there would be a twinkle. So you'd kind of know she quite liked you, really, but she was keeping you a bit at arm's length."

John's mother Julia, above, turned him over at age 5 to the care of her elder sister, Mimi, who raised him in an upscale house on Liverpool's Menlove Avenue.

Known as the Silver Beetles in early 1960, the band acquires bassist Stu Sutcliffe, far left, and has Johnny Hutch sitting in on drums. By August, it is bound for Hamburg.

It was complicated. Part of it would have been class snobbery, which in England has always fed on the subtlest social gradations. But to a certain extent, the prim Mimi kept everyone at arm's length, even her beloved nephew. At the same time, John could also make her melt: after his first guitar broke, she bought him his second, a prized Hofner Club 40. He was a brilliant, confused, angry boy—angry at the father who had run off to sea when John was 4, and at his adored mother who'd given him up and then had two children with another man. And he grew all the angrier after Julia was killed. "I lost my mother twice," John said, years later. "Once as a child of 5 and then again at 17. It made me very, very bitter inside."

"John had an acerbic wit, and he'd pull people down—if he could humiliate you, he did," Bill Harry says. "Paul was the gentleman, always kind and considerate to people. I think that was the upbringing that his father gave him."

In fact, Paul McCartney had his own demons, but he kept them to himself. He was tough underneath the gentlemanly exterior: the hyper-perceptive Lennon would have seen at once that he couldn't pull him down, and would have respected this as much as he respected the younger boy's superior musicianship. And sweetening the deal was the fact that they shared an absurd (and sometimes cruel) sense of humor: Paul and John both loved *The Goon Show,* the Spike Milligan and Peter Sellers radio program whose off-the-wall comedy paved the way for Monty Python.

But first came the music. They fitted together, hand in glove: John's anger, natural rebelliousness ("He decided very early on that he didn't like doing as he was told," recalls Quarrymen bandmate Rod Davis) and more limited technical ability made him a dyed-in-the-wool rock 'n' roller. Paul, too, loved Little Richard and Elvis and Gene Vincent, but his anger was buried deeper, and he had grown up listening to, and loving, old standards at family musicales. His palette was broader.

Strange (but then again, not so strange) that the boy with the posh upbringing would wind up as the world's Working-Class Hero, while the boy from the council flats would become the fabulously wealthy Sir Paul, writer of silly love songs and oratorios.

PLAYING DANCE-HALL GIGS around Liverpool, the guitar trio—sometimes still billed as the Quarrymen, at least once appearing as Johnny and the Moondogs—picked up drummers wherever they could. Then, in January 1960, they acquired a bassist.

Stuart Sutcliffe was a classmate and close friend of John's at the Liverpool College of Art: a delicate young man, elfin-handsome, with rich potential as a painter and no discernible ability as a musician. But Sutcliffe looked the part, with his brooding resemblance to James Dean and his dark sunglasses, even if all he could play on the bass was an off-key *thunk-thunk-thunk-thunk.*

And along with a bassist, the freshly minted foursome acquired a new name, invented after a night of brainstorming on the part of Lennon and Sutcliffe: the Beatals.

It seemed perfect, at once punning on Buddy Holly's Crickets, name-checking Jack Kerouac's Beat Generation and paying homage to the rock-'n'-roll rhythms that had crossed the Atlantic and taken Liverpool by storm. Rock bands were springing up all over the Merseyside: Gerry and the Pacemakers, Cass & the Casanovas, Derry and the Seniors, Rory Storm and the Hurricanes. In the spring of 1960, a London impresario named Larry Parnes came to Liverpool to audition backup bands for a summer Scottish tour by two of his acts, newly minted rockers stage-named Duffy Power and Johnny Gentle. He chose Cass & the Casanovas to play behind Duffy Power, and John, Paul, George and Stu—still just a cover band with no original material and known, for reasons too abstruse to go into, as the Silver Beetles—to back Johnny Gentle.

"Now we were truly professional," Paul recalled. "[And] we could do something we had been toying with for a long time, which was to change our names to real show-biz names. I became Paul Ramon, which I thought was suitably exotic."

The Scottish tour was a fiasco. "We were playing to nobody in little halls," George Harrison remembered. "Our shoes were full of holes, and our trousers were a mess, while Johnny Gentle had a posh suit … The band was horrible, an embarrassment. We didn't have amplifiers or anything."

Still, with every show, they learned. Back in Liverpool, in August, they scuffled around for gigs, like the one they got at a strip club (Paul sat in on drums) at which the stripper handed the boys the sheet music for her act: "Gypsy Fire Dance." Wrong boys. These four couldn't read music. Instead, they played Duane Eddy's "Ramrod" and—no doubt at Paul's suggestion—the romantic old big-band number "Moonglow."

Over the summer, the boys dropped "Silver" from the band's name and returned to their roots by re-spelling *Beetles* as *Beatles.* The world was unimpressed. Gigs were few and far between; hope flickered low. "Then," McCartney recalled, "Hamburg came up."

IN AUGUST OF 1960, Paul McCartney was at a crossroads. He had just turned 18, and he was trying to figure out what to do with the rest of his life. Rather, he knew what he wanted to do with his life but wasn't sure if he could afford it. Unlike Lennon, who was in the process of flunking out of the Liverpool College of Art (and didn't much care), McCartney was a planner. And since he now saw his life options narrowing, he was thinking seriously about applying to teachers college.

That was when Allan Williams entered the picture. Williams, who owned a Liverpool coffee shop and student hangout called the Jacaranda, managed Derry and the Seniors. Hearing that nightclubs in the rough-and-tumble German port city of Hamburg were eager to sign English

Paul with his father, Jim, and brother Mike in 1960, the year Paul turns 18 and the Beatles turn a corner.

rock groups, Williams went over to investigate and met a colorful club owner named Bruno Koschmider. Soon Derry and the Seniors were playing in Koschmider's club, the Kaiserkeller, where they were such a success that the German asked Williams if he had any more bands to send over.

The trick wasn't getting the Beatles to agree; it was persuading their parents. After the death of his mother, John was living on his own. But Harrison, at 17, was officially underage, and even Paul needed his father's signature on the contract. Jim McCartney, thinking about his late wife, felt she would have wanted Paul to continue his education. But, Paul recalled, "we were told, 'You can go to Hamburg and get £15 a week.' Now £15 a week was more than my dad earned. In fact, the teachers at school didn't earn more than that … I remember writing to my headmaster very proudly that summer: 'I am sure you will understand why I will not be coming back in September.'

"I remember Dad giving me lots of advice," Paul said, "but there was an agreement that he had to sign … This was The Big Thing."

There was also the small matter of a drummer: they still didn't have one. But then someone remembered that Pete Best, the handsome son of the Casbah's owner, had gotten a drum kit for Christmas and seemed to bang on it reasonably skillfully. Would Pete like to accompany them to Hamburg? He would.

And so on Aug. 16, 1960, the Beatles, now a fivesome, met at the Jacaranda, piled into Allan Williams' van—"I drove them to Hamburg because they were that broke," Williams recalls—and rode off to meet their future.

SCOTLAND WAS A Sunday-school picnic by comparison. The St. Pauli district of Hamburg was Sin City itself, jammed with garish nightclubs, legalized bordellos and sex shops. Prostitutes—women, or men who looked like women—sat in windows, displaying their wares. St. Pauli's main stem was the infamous Reeperbahn; Bruno Koschmider's Kaiserkeller was on an equally seamy thoroughfare nearby called Grosse Freiheit—Great Freedom.

The five young men were all in favor of great freedom: none of them were prudes. They weren't even especially thrown by the accommodations the club owner provided: a reeking, windowless storage room behind the movie screen in a porn theater called the Bambi Kino.

The worst shock was the work schedule. The Beatles were required to play seven days a week—four and a half hours a night, from Monday to Friday, six hours on Saturday and Sunday. It was an exhausting grind in two ways: for one thing, the band knew only about 15 songs, or roughly a half-hour's worth of material. To stretch out what they had, they would play extended jams—Ray Charles' "What'd I Say" was a favorite.

But the sheer grind of playing and singing for hour after hour, as loudly as possible to be heard over the drunken patrons, took its toll, even on energetic young men. Soon, some of the group started taking diet pills—Preludins—to keep going, along with the beer and watered Scotch and Cokes they drank on the house. John, wound up on pills, would often vent his cruel sense of humor, shouting obscenities at the audience, yelling, '*Heil,* Hitler!', once even coming onstage wearing a toilet seat around his neck. The boozed-up clientele loved it.

Klaus Voormann wasn't a regular patron but rather a 22-year-old Hamburg art student who discovered the Beatles quite by accident. One night, after a fight with his girlfriend, he walked to St. Pauli to cool off; hearing some intriguing-sounding music coming from a club, he went in

and was dazzled. He'd never been interested in rock 'n' roll before, and here it was, alive and thrilling. He brought back his girlfriend, Astrid Kirchherr, along with another friend, Jürgen Vollmer, to hear the wild young Englishmen.

The young Germans soon attached themselves to the band, and a certain cross-fertilization began, the Liverpudlians taking to wearing black leather and letting their hair grow scruffy in imitation of their new friends. The slim, blond Kirchherr took haunting black-and-white photographs of John, Paul and George—Pete, who lacked the quick wit of the others, didn't quite fit in—and fell in love with the doomed Sutcliffe, who would die of a brain hemorrhage in 1962.

Both Voormann and Kirchherr took note of McCartney's performing style. "I remember Paul very much because he was the one that was most forward onstage," Voormann, now 73, told TIME. "He was using all the German he could remember from school, talking to the audience in German. 'Hello—*Wie gehts?*' and 'Next number—*das nächste Stuck.*'"

"He was jumping up and down and pulling faces when he was singing and shook his head," Kirchherr told Howard Sounes, author of *Fab: An Intimate Life of Paul McCartney.* "The only one who was a professional entertainer was Paul."

But in his visits to the Kaiserkeller, Voormann also noticed the rivalry between Lennon and McCartney. "That came across onstage all the time," he recalls. "A constant competition going on, even to the point that sometimes Paul wanted to do a song, and John said, 'No, fuck, I'm going to do this [other] song.' Paul gave in very quickly in those days. Later on, he didn't. But then he just let John sing the song."

Another form of competition occurred at the Kaiserkeller: an ongoing battle of the bands, in alternating sets, between the Beatles, and Derry and the Seniors, and then with the newly arrived Rory Storm and the Hurricanes, whose drummer, Ritchie Starkey—stage-named Ringo Starr—was miles ahead of Pete Best. The face-off forced Lennon, McCartney and Harrison to build their repertoire exponentially, learning entire LPs by Chuck Berry, Elvis, Gene Vincent and—thanks to a new (and far more experienced) musical friend, Tony Sheridan, a bad-boy

On its first trip to Hamburg, in 1960, the band, now called the Beatles, takes on a harder look and sound, as well as rowdy new fans and an entourage of young Germans that includes photographer Astrid Kirchherr, who chronicles its rise with moody shots like these, above and below, at the Hamburg fairground.

singer-guitarist headlining at the Top Ten club—R&B tunes by the likes of Jimmy Reed, T-Bone Walker and John Lee Hooker. Tightened and toughened, the Beatles could soon play two- and three-hour sets effortlessly. Hamburg, their crucible, turned them from a larking bunch of amateurs into a real rock-'n'-roll band.

AND YET EVEN AS THEY CAME together, they almost fell apart. In a random check of papers, the Hamburg police discovered that George was a minor and sent him packing back to Liverpool. Without a lead guitarist, the band decided the only option was to quit the Kaiserkeller and back Sheridan at the Top Ten. Furious, Koschmider terminated the contracts—and the work permits—of John, Paul, Pete and Stu. Moving their belongings from the Bambi Kino in the middle of the night, Paul and Pete lit some matches to see (in fact, with the wisdom of youth, they used condoms as torches) and accidentally (or maybe not so acci-

Sutcliffe looks the part, and falls in love with Kirchherr, but before long, his incompetence on bass costs him his job.

dentally) started a small fire. In any case, Koschmider had them arrested, and they were taken to the airport in handcuffs. It would not be McCartney's last arrest.

Without permits, John and Stu had no option but to straggle back home. The Beatles were in disarray, all but defunct. Jim McCartney told his wayward son that the jig was up; it was time to get a job, any job. And the chastened Paul complied, taking a £7-a-week sweeping-up position at a Liverpool electrical-wire factory.

And then, just like that, the band came back together. A local emcee/deejay named Bob Wooler, hearing of its success in Germany, booked it for a dance-hall gig in a Liverpool suburb. "The Beatles—Direct from Hamburg," the ad copy read. At first, fans thought they were German: with their black leather jackets and tight, hard sound, the boys didn't remotely resemble any of the local bands. They caught on fast. In a quick reversal of fortune, the Beatles became the hottest thing in northern England. And they got only hotter when Wooler began featuring them at the lunchtime concerts he hosted at the Cavern, a tiny, dank, underground club in downtown Liverpool. It was here, in the proverbial Cellarful of Noise, where performers stood virtually in the audience, that the Beatles first truly bonded with their fans: girls who wanted to be with them, boys who wanted to be them.

THE BAND RETURNED to Hamburg in the spring of 1961 (George had turned 18; Paul and Pete managed to clear up their little police matter with letters of apology), no longer beginners. The boys opened for and sometimes backed Tony Sheridan, singing harmony and projecting electrifying (and Preludin-fueled) energy, wowing the crowds at the Top Ten and the Star Club. John's girlfriend Cynthia came over to visit, along with Paul's hometown girl Dot Rhone, whom he'd also met at the Casbah. Dot was thrilled when Paul gave her an engagement ring, but also wondered whether Paul was growing away from her. Something was in the air, a feeling that the Beatles were about to happen.

Some kind of reckoning where their weakest musical link was concerned was inevitable.

One night onstage, Paul—sick of Stu's incompetence on bass and probably jealous of his friendship with John—made a nasty crack about Astrid. Sutcliffe dropped his bass and slugged him. A wild fistfight between the two ensued, and by the end of the week, Stu announced he was returning to art school. He was through with the Beatles. Paul inherited his bass.

In August, the band accompanied Tony Sheridan on a commercial record date, the group's first. They were thrilled. The LP, larded with old-fashioned numbers like "Ain't She Sweet" and "The Saints," included a version of "My Bonnie" that started slow and sentimental and turned into a rocking rave-up. The German label Polydor released the song as a single, and though the Beatles were barely recognizable on the track, it was the record that lit the fuse of their career.

[CHAPTER 2]

Mersey!

THE CAVERN WAS WELL NAMED: a claustrophobe's nightmare; a tiny, reeking, stone-walled pit of a club two stories below narrow Mathew Street in downtown Liverpool. The air stank of stale cigarette smoke; the damp walls seeped and dripped an unholy ooze onto the customers' heads. The echo was good, though. A hundred or more people at a time would crowd in on

weekend evenings or during the club's lunch-hour concerts, and the crowds had been grow-ing since early 1961, when the place switched from a traditional-jazz format, which had been drawing an ever-diminishing clientele of politely dressed college students and young adults, to rock 'n' roll, which had nothing to do with politeness.

The Beatles (the group's name was only six months old then) had first played the Cavern as neophytes, in February 1961, before heading back for a second stand in Hamburg, the riotous port city where they'd served a kind of apprenticeship the previous year. Their second trip to Hamburg forged them into a great band. One of their biggest fans was the drummer for rival group Rory Storm and the Hurricanes. "We played the same club every night, and we got to know each other," Ringo Starr told TIME. "On the weekend, we did 12 hours between the two bands, which is quite a stretch. If they had the last session, I would just sit there [and watch]. I just loved that front line. I loved John, George and Paul. I thought that was the best front line around."

A lot of people felt the same. After the second Hamburg trip, the Beatles returned to Liver-pool in triumph, filled with confidence. "What we generated was fantastic, when we played straight rock," John Lennon recalled. "There was nobody to touch us in Britain."

Their appeal went beyond music. With their black leather outfits and their constant, con-fident joking onstage—although the "moody, magnificent" Pete, so dubbed by Cavern deejay Bob Wooler, didn't say much—they had charisma. And something else. "They had a great rap-port with the fans," Bill Harry says. "They used to chat onstage, take requests from the girls. The girls would come in with their hair in curlers with these scarves on and sit down in the front row, waiting, while the other groups came and went. Then, just before the Beatles came on, they'd all take their curlers out and do their hair in the front row."

"We did well at the Cavern, attracted some big audiences, and word got around," Paul McCartney said. One of the people word got around to was Brian Epstein.

ON THE FACE OF IT, the 27-year-old Epstein was the last person who would have been interested in the Beatles or any other rock-'n'-roll band, despite the fact that he ran the record department at the Whitechapel branch of his family's business, North End Music Store (NEMS), just a couple of hundred yards from the Cavern. (Jim McCartney had bought the family's upright piano from NEMS on an easy-payment plan years before.) Epstein, whose musical tastes ran to classical, thought rock was just noise. He was an ultra-refined young man, perfectly dressed at all times and armored with a slightly haughty manner and a posh accent far removed from Liverpool's nasal, ironic twang. His self-protective snobbery compensated for a certain shame at being Jewish in a country that still harbored much anti-Semitism—and, more deeply, for the fact that he was gay.

Despite Epstein's own musical tastes, his business interests were piqued in late October 1961 when teenagers started coming into the shop asking for a record called "My Bonnie," fea-turing a group called the Beatles. In reminiscences recorded years later, Epstein professed never to have heard of these Beatles. But according to biographer Bob Spitz, the record merchant would likely have been well aware of the group through Bill Harry's rock newspaper, *Mersey Beat,* which was featuring the Beatles extensively that fall and selling briskly in NEMS—not to mention through their occasional visits to the store, during which they lingered in the listen-ing booths, jotting down the lyrics to the latest Chuck Berry or Little Richard but rarely buying anything. More likely, Epstein, whose life was layered with secrets, had noticed the handsome, leather-clad young men and taken a fancy to them. And when a woman he knew said, "The

In 1963, Beatles manager Brian Epstein is at the Cavern Club (during a performance by another band). There, two years earlier, he first witnessed the Beatles and told his assistant, "I think they're tremendous." Epstein got them a record deal and gave them a complete image makeover.

Beatles? They're the greatest. They're at the Cavern this week," the record merchant, who had ambitions beyond his father's music store, needed no prodding to go see for himself.

The date was Nov. 9, 1961: a Thursday noontime. The Cavern was jammed with students and young officeworkers on lunch break. Epstein and his assistant Alistair Taylor—only in their late 20s but, in their ties and jackets, looking ages older than everyone else—sat stiffly in the back of the dank little grotto, appalled by what they saw and heard. "The place was packed, and steam was rolling down the walls," Taylor told Spitz many years later. "The music was so loud, we couldn't hear ourselves think." And the Beatles? "They were deafening," Taylor recalled. "And so unprofessional—laughing with the girls, smoking onstage and sipping from Cokes during their act. But absolutely magic! The vibe they generated was just unbelievable."

After the set, Epstein and Taylor stopped by the club's tiny band room to introduce themselves to the boys, then went to lunch. Epstein asked his assistant what he thought of the band, and Taylor said that though the music had sounded awful to him, there was something remarkable about the whole scene—both the crowd's fervor and the band's energy. Epstein seemed barely able to contain himself. Finally, he said, "I think they're tremendous!" Then he grabbed Taylor by the arm. "Do you think I should manage them?" he asked.

THE BEATLES MAY HAVE BEEN a great rock band in those early days, but in show-business terms, they were rank amateurs—as was Brian Epstein, who understood the business of selling records in a shop but not much else. "I will never know," Epstein wrote in his memoirs, "what made me say to this eccentric group of boys that I thought a further meeting might be helpful to them and me."

The boys resisted. Of the four, Paul McCartney was the most skeptical about their would-be manager. Uncharacteristically, McCartney was an hour late to their first official business meeting, in early December, because, George Harrison reported after phoning his house, he had just gotten up and was taking a bath. "This is disgraceful!" cried the tightly wound Epstein. "He's very late!"

"And very clean," said George.

Finally, Paul arrived, and as he later recalled, "We went upstairs to Brian's office to make the deal. I was talking to him, trying to beat him down, knowing the game: try to get the manager to take a low percentage. And the others tried as well, but he stuck at a figure of 25%. [In fact, in the end, Epstein came down to 20%.] He told us, 'That'll do, now I'll be your manager,' and we agreed."

Epstein, to his credit, was fair enough to insist that he wouldn't sign their representation agreement until he had secured the group a record contract. This would prove to be easier said than done. Epstein first approached EMI, the biggest record company in Britain, with "My Bonnie." Not interested, EMI sniffed. The manager then got the boys an audition with Decca, in London, on New Year's Day, 1962.

It was the Beatles' first trip to the big city—which was notoriously snobbish about northerners like them—and they stayed out late celebrating New Year's, finally grabbing a couple hours' sleep at their cheap hotel before stumbling over to the Decca Studios the next morning to record their audition. They were not only exhausted but terrified. And though they loosened up over the course of 15 songs—a motley assortment of corny standards ("The Sheik of Araby," "September in the Rain," "Besame Mucho"), rockers ("Memphis," "Money," "Three Cool Cats") and three early Lennon-McCartney originals ("Hello Little Girl," "Like Dreamers Do," "Love of the Loved")—they never came close, in the cold recording studio, to capturing their electrifying potential.

Paul, in London in 1963, when the band hits No. 1 in Britain for the first time. With it comes the beginning of Beatlemania.

Decca passed. The higher-ups there, the label's A&R head, Dick Rowe, told Epstein, "didn't like the boys' sound." Besides, Rowe said, "groups with guitars are on the way out." The coming thing, he informed the manager, was teen idols like Frankie Avalon, Bobby Darin and Dion.

In truth, nobody really knew in early 1962 what the coming thing was. In a period when Elvis, the man who had shaken up the world with his wild music, was busily cranking out sappy movies, it seemed to Lennon, McCartney and Harrison as though even rock 'n' roll might be a passing fancy. Paul, though, had broader musical interests. "I could never see the difference between a beautiful melody and a cool rock-'n'-roll song," he recalled.

"Paul was always charming, and he was an incredible singer," Ringo Starr says. "He had many voices. He could sing like Little Richard, but he could also sing Fats Waller songs, country songs. He was very versatile."

He also had the kind of drive that none of the others possessed. As McCartney told Epstein after the Beatles signed the management contract, he hoped the Beatles would succeed. "But I'll tell you now, Mr. Epstein, I'm going to be a star anyway."

The Beatles had widened Epstein's horizons. Their humor, inventive flair and irresistible personalities infused the music with a charm that had previously eluded the manager. And there was something else: John Lennon and Paul McCartney were beginning to write songs together, and that fact, along with the songs themselves, interested Epstein.

Most of the original numbers weren't very good at first—Paul later called "Like Dreamers Do,"

The Beatles, with their new suits and haircuts in 1963, are restyled.
Manager Epstein has "changed the group from John Lennon's into Paul
McCartney's. He completely smoothed them out."

one of the three the group played for the Decca audition, "really bad." But even a song this weak, he noticed, had an interesting effect when the band dared to play it at the Cavern: "It was enough," McCartney recalled. "We rehearsed it and played it, and the kids liked it because they had never heard it before. It was something they could only hear when they came to see our show.

"Looking back," Paul said, "we were putting it all together very cleverly, albeit instinctively. We were making ourselves into a group that was different."

Whatever spark they had, though, was lost on the record companies. Then, just when it seemed no label in England would go near them, merest chance led Epstein back to EMI—and not to the front office but to the obscure producer in charge of one of the company's minor divisions, Parlophone.

George Martin was a walking contradiction: an aristocratically handsome, classically trained musician (oboe, piano) whose chief stock in trade was comedy. He had turned Parlophone into a minor cash cow for EMI by recording major English comic acts such as the Beyond the Fringe troupe (Jonathan Miller, Peter Cook and Dudley Moore) and the great Peter Sellers. But comedy had a limited shelf life. The musician in Martin wanted to be involved with music, and the businessman in him was looking for something with earning power. What that meant in the early '60s was pop.

A string of lucky accidents led the Beatles to Martin. After the Decca audition, Epstein had encountered a London music publisher who was intrigued with the idea of acquiring the rights to the original songs of Lennon and McCartney. But, Epstein explained to the publisher, since the boys performed their own material, it wouldn't be worth much unless they had a record deal. The publisher put Epstein in touch with Martin.

And Martin listened to the Decca tape and was unimpressed. Still, something about the vocals—Paul's charm blending with John's roughness—caught his ear. He told Epstein he would give the boys a listen in person.

In the meantime, Epstein—for no great profit at first—threw himself into managing his enthralling quartet. The first item of business was a complete image makeover. It was time, the manager told the Beatles, to stop acting like amateurs and look, and behave, like a professional act. This meant no more eating, drinking or smoking onstage— but that was only the beginning.

George Martin, a classically trained musician and an obscure producer at a label known mostly for comedy albums, is an unlikely candidate to sign the Beatles.

"Epstein changed the group from John Lennon's group into Paul McCartney's," Bill Harry says. "First, he said, 'You've got to get rid of the black leathers,' and he took them to Beno Dorn, his tailor, to make them mohair suits. He took them to Horne Brothers, the hairdressers at the corner of Lord Street, and had their hair done. He took them to the Empire Theater to watch the Shadows, who bowed at the end of their act, and [he said], 'That's what you've got to do.'

"He completely smoothed them out, to John's fury. John and Pete Best didn't really want to give up their leathers. But Brian changed them completely—made them go onstage all dressed properly and all the rest of it. As a rebel, John used to unfasten the top button of his shirt, so Paul would tie his tie up again for him. Because Paul was delighted. This was what Paul wanted. This was the way to go."

THE BOYS WORE TIES to the audition at EMI's tony Abbey Road studios on June 6, 1962, and George Martin was charmed by their enthusiasm and natural wit (though, as always, the silent Pete Best was odd man out); it was their music that was problematic.

Martin was underwhelmed by the old standards that Paul fronted—"Besame Mucho," Fats Waller's "Your Feet's Too Big"; and the Lennon-McCartney originals they performed—"Love

Me Do," "Please Please Me," "Ask Me Why"—weren't clicking. The producer saw potential, but there was a serious problem. "George took us to one side and said, 'I'm really unhappy with the drummer. Would you consider changing him?'" Paul recalled.

"We said, 'No, we can't!' It was one of those terrible things you go through as kids. Can we betray him? No. But our career was on the line. Maybe they were going to cancel our contract."

As it turned out, Parlophone offered the group a contract—not a very long-lasting or lucrative one (one year; a penny royalty per disc), but a contract. The group had just made it in the door on the strength of their charm and musical spark, but on each count, they had a liability, and that liability was one and the same person.

The ax fell on Pete Best a few weeks later; the executioner was Brian Epstein. "They don't think you're a good enough drummer, Pete," the manager told Best. "And George Martin doesn't think you're a good enough drummer." As Best stammered a defense, Epstein's phone rang. It was Paul, calling to make sure the deed had been done.

McCartney had been conflicted in Hamburg about the doomed Stu Sutcliffe (who died that April of a sudden brain hemorrhage), not only because the unmusical Sutcliffe was dragging the band down with his limited bass playing but also out of jealousy of Stu's close friendship with John. And then there was the issue of Sutcliffe's good looks—Paul felt that was his department.

Pete Best had two of the same three problems, as far as McCartney was concerned. First, and most grievous, his drumming was demonstrably handicapping the band. But the way the girls screamed for Pete also did nothing to endear him to Paul, who shed no tears at his ouster. "Pete Best was good but a bit limited," he said.

The girls felt otherwise. On Aug. 19, 1962, when the Beatles gave their first Cavern performance with their new drummer—the best in Liverpool, agreed John, Paul and George, who felt lucky to have snatched Ritchie Starkey away from Rory Storm and the Hurricanes—the outraged female fans started chanting: "Pete forever! Ringo never!"

But the chanting would soon be drowned out by gales of fresh screaming.

THE SAME AUGUST WEEK marked another personnel change for Paul McCartney, one that would have been far more pleasing to the group's female fans had they known anything about it: he ended his two-and-a-half-year relationship with his hometown girlfriend Dot Rhone. She was three months' pregnant with their child when she miscarried that July; until then, the two had been seriously planning to get married—Paul had even taken out a license. Now he broke it all off, with visibly mixed feelings.

"He seemed upset," Rhone recalled many years later, "but deep down, he was probably relieved."

Ironically, one of the tracks the Beatles laid down just a couple of weeks later, at the group's first recording session for George Martin and Parlophone, a McCartney original called "P.S. I Love You," had been inspired by the love letters Paul wrote Dot from Hamburg. But this song was relegated to the B-side of the single that resulted from the session; the A-side was a revamped version of "Love Me Do."

Released in October, the catchy, blues-harmonica-driven tune went to No. 17 on the British charts. Then, at the end of November, the Beatles returned to Abbey Road studios and recorded another original called "Please Please Me."

The song rocked from the beginning to the end of its two minutes and one second, propelled by John's hoarsely insistent lead vocal, Paul's melodic bass, the front line's perfect three-part harmonies and Ringo's poundingly inventive backbeat. For the first time, the group had

When the bandmates record "Please, Please Me," Martin tells them, "You've just made your first No. 1 record." He is right.

truly come together as a group, every component working perfectly, blending perfectly. When the last chord faded, George Martin, grinning, clicked on the intercom in the control booth. "Gentlemen," he said, "you've just made your first No. 1 record."

And so the madness began.

NOT ONLY DID "PLEASE PLEASE ME" go to No. 1 in Britain, so also did the Beatles' first album, named after the single and recorded—14 songs in all—on one incredible day in February 1963. "That's where they wanted to be—No. 1; but with it came the beginning of Beatlemania," recalled the group's roadie, driver and friend Neil Aspinall. "They'd had a lot of madness in Liverpool, but they knew all the kids there. They didn't try to jump on you or overturn the van or rip the wing mirrors off. Suddenly this absolute craziness was going on, which was very exciting but difficult to deal with."

Suddenly the Fab Four—the nickname was coined by their new PR man Tony Barrow—were wanted everywhere, and they obliged with concerts and personal appearances up and down Britain. They were usually on a bill with other performers, but more and more frequently through that amazing year, the other acts became asterisks, afterthoughts, interchangeable: in the middle of their sets, the audience would start calling for the Beatles.

Something gigantic had come unbottled. The Beatles, looking like no one else in their mop-top haircuts and collarless suits, and sounding like no one else amid a sea of insipid pop, were an antidote—to the dreary repression and poverty of postwar England, to British manners and class snobbery, to age and conformity. The Beatles were an elixir, and it seemed all of England was drunk on them.

When *A Hard Day's Night* premieres, in July 1964 in London, fans hoping to catch a glimpse of the group stage exactly the kind of delirious scene that the movie chronicles.

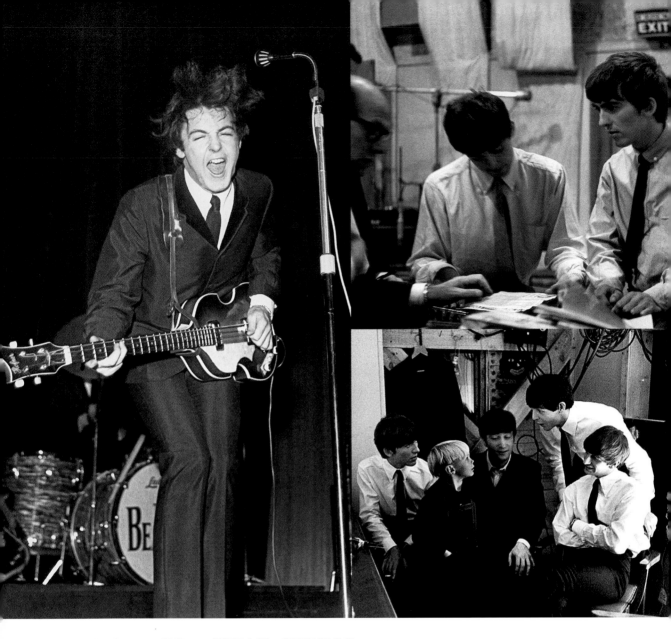

The breakout year, 1963, clockwise from above: Paul wigs out on a U.K. tour; the band signs documents at Abbey Road studios; Paul and George catch news and a smoke backstage; a lucky boy gets to meet the Fab Four before a Stockholm TV appearance.

THAT SPRING, the group topped the bill at a pop show in London's grandest concert venue, the Royal Albert Hall, where the screams were as loud as they'd been at the Cavern. After the show, Paul spotted a particularly interesting-looking girl backstage—a striking redhead, very young but very self-possessed, who'd been sent by the BBC's radio magazine to review the concert. Just 17, Jane Asher was a celebrity in her own right: a TV and movie actress since the age of 5 and a well-known young woman about town. She was well spoken and forthright: she hadn't thought much of the other bands on the bill, she said—"noisy" was her verdict—but the Beatles had impressed her.

Paul McCartney was also impressed. And then more impressed after he and Jane began dating and he met her remarkable family. Her mother was a professional oboist (who, amazingly, had taught George Martin); her father, a prominent psychiatrist and a published writer;

older brother Peter and younger sister Claire, also redheads, accomplished actors and musicians. (Peter had already formed a singing duo, Peter & Gordon, with school friend Gordon Waller, and the two would become a highly successful act in the '60s with the No. 1 hit "A World Without Love"—written by Paul McCartney.) The whole family was musical, literary, intellectual and magnetic, and they lived in a big town house on Wimpole Street, just across the way from poet Elizabeth Barrett Browning's girlhood home.

"I would imagine we must have been somewhat intimidating," Peter Asher said recently. "But Paul's not easily cowed by people, and he counts on his very considerable charm, which works. He's a super-amiable, charming man—and very clever."

Still, the Ashers represented something that the working-class boy from Liverpool, for all his own brilliance and early success, wanted badly. "He felt it important to be in the center of things," Tony Barrow told McCartney biographer Howard Sounes. "And that's where Jane Asher came in ... being not just the girlfriend but somebody who could lift him up that social ladder ... He felt that she would be helpful to him and useful to him in progressing his march up through London society."

The two were a serious item from the start. "I have always been someone who gets into a steady relationship," Paul has said. Jane made the trip to Liverpool for Paul's 21st birthday party, on June 18, 1963—a significant gesture. And it was a significant party, not only because it marked Paul's transition to adulthood but also because of a fistfight that broke out.

Always prickly under the best of conditions, John Lennon had been feeling edgy about the direction the Beatles were going in. "John was getting very, very disenchanted," Bill Harry says, about the show-biz style that Brian Epstein had pressed on them—and Paul had eagerly adopted. And so, when Epstein, who happened to be in love with Lennon, invited him along on a weekend trip to Barcelona, John went. Paul's take on the trip: "John saw his opportunity to impress upon Mr. Epstein who was the boss of the group—I think that's why he went on holiday with Brian."

At the birthday party, though, Cavern deejay Bob Wooler puckishly asked Lennon how his "honeymoon" with Epstein had gone. Lennon exploded, fisticuffs ensued, and the party ended in chaos. John may have defended his straight credentials, but he had lost the battle with Brian and Paul. The Beatles would be all show-biz for the rest of their concert days—and rather successful at it, too.

"We make more money out of writing songs," John later said, somewhat defensively, "than we do out of appearing and running round waving and that." But with Lennon and McCartney, the sheer joy of songwriting preceded everything, including money. "Paul *loved* working with John," Bob Spitz says. "At the beginning it was like sex—they popped them off, one after another."

In his book, Spitz quotes a singer named Kenny Lynch, who toured with the Beatles in England that year: "They wrote every day on the coach, like clockwork." "At some point," Spitz writes, "John or Paul would catch the other's eye, then they would get up nonchalantly, work their way to the back of the bus, take out their guitars and get down to business ... They were in their own private world back there, absorbed by the instant gratification of the work and adept at blocking out distractions. Every so often, Kenny would lean over the seat in front of them and attempt to offer a line or critique the work. 'Fuck off! Turn around!' they replied—and they meant it."

"Crediting the songs jointly to Lennon and McCartney was a decision we made very early on because we aspired to be Rodgers and Hammerstein," said Paul—who nevertheless bridled at the Lennon/McCartney label. "I wanted it to be 'McCartney/Lennon,'" he said, "but John had the stronger personality, and I think he fixed things with Brian ... That was John's way."

Paul was spending more and more time in London. And that fall, in an unusual arrangement, he moved into the Ashers' house on Wimpole Street, occupying—when he wasn't on the road—an attic bedroom across from the room of Jane's brother Peter. "I would borrow records from him because he had cool R&B records that I did not have," Peter remembers. "He played the guitar a lot and then wrote sometimes up there. Then, famously, of course, they wrote 'I Want to Hold Your Hand' in the basement."

"I remember when we got the chord that made that song," Lennon recalled. "We were in Jane Asher's house, downstairs in the cellar, playing on the piano at the same time, and we had, 'Oh, you-u-u ... got that something ...' And Paul hits this chord, and I turn to him and say, 'That's it! Do that again!' In those days, we really used to absolutely write like that—both playing into each other's noses."

THE BEATLES HAD FOUR NO. 1 singles in Britain in 1963, and two No. 1 albums (their second, *With The Beatles,* came out that fall). Beatlemania gripped the sceptered isle, and still the U.S. barely knew of the group's existence.

By mid-November, the three American TV networks were getting wind of this quaint hysteria and sent camera crews to cover a Beatles concert at a theater in the south of England. Film clips came back to the States, but by then few took notice—especially after the national tragedy that gripped the country on Nov. 22, 1963.

Americans stumbled on after the assassination of President John F. Kennedy, and three weeks later, a Washington disc jockey took a request from a teenager who'd seen an odd English band on TV. The deejay, Carroll James, tracked down an import copy of the Beatles' latest hit, "I Want to Hold Your Hand," and played it on his WWDC show. Minutes later, the station's switchboard lit up.

In late December, Capitol Records released "I Want to Hold Your Hand" in the U.S. Two weeks later, the Beatles were playing the Olympia Theater in Paris. "One night," Paul recalled, "we arrived back at the hotel from the Olympia, when a telegram came through to Brian from Capitol Records ... He came running into the room saying, 'Hey, look! You are No. 1 in America!'"

WE WERE A DIFFERENT COUNTRY then, a more unified one in many ways, and we gathered around our black-and-white televisions for certain important events: space shots, Inaugurations, the yearly showing of *The Wizard of Oz.* In late November 1963, the whole country joined in mourning and disbelief, watching the aftermath of the Kennedy assassination, transfixed in front of our TV sets for days at a time.

The Ed Sullivan Show, on Sunday nights, was a television ritual for millions of families. And on Feb. 9, 1964, the largest audience ever recorded for an American television program, 73 million viewers in more than 23 million households, watched that broadcast with another kind of disbelief, as the four young Englishmen with outrageously long hair—having just stepped off a plane two days earlier at New York City's newly renamed John F. Kennedy International Airport—sang in close, high harmonies, seemingly having the time of their lives, while the young girls in the studio audience wept and screamed in a joyous, helplessly desirous frenzy.

America changed forever in that less-than-three-month span at the end of '63 and the beginning of '64. A certain innocence was lost and a certain new kind of innocence gained, as the Beatles made many Americans—and especially young Americans—feel that hope and happiness, and perhaps even something beyond happiness, might be possible again. "I think they helped lift up the great wounded beast that was America after the President was killed," the theater and movie director Michael Lindsay-Hogg, who would work closely with the group and then with McCartney a few years later, told TIME.

And in return, America would lift the Beatles to heights even they couldn't have imagined.

IN THE SPRING OF 1964, the Beatles made a movie, and though there were a million ways it could have gone wrong, *A Hard Day's Night* turned out miraculously right. A lot of the credit goes to its ground-breaking young director, Richard Lester, whom Lennon and McCartney instantly chose when they heard he had directed *The Running Jumping & Standing Still Film,* a plotless comic short starring two of their heroes, Spike Milligan and Peter Sellers. *A Hard Day's Night* (the title came from one of Ringo's winsome malapropisms) didn't have much standing still, but the black-and-white pseudo-documentary, which followed the Beatles on tour in London and environs, had a lot of running, as the four tried to evade hordes of screaming girls. The film also had a baker's dozen of original new songs and a huge amount of charm.

At first glance, Paul may have seemed—as he was onstage—the most camera-ready of the four, the most ingratiating and show-biz-y performer, but thanks to Lester's willingness to let the camera run and make the most of semi-improvised scenes (the screenplay was by Welsh playwright Alun Owen), each of the Beatles came across equally well. Though they had never acted before, they all gave off the same comic charisma onscreen that had won over George Martin: they were just being themselves, four cheeky lads from Liverpool, and it worked.

A Hard Day's Night was a sheer shot of joy—it made everything the Beatles did, even touring, look like fun—and it was just what the doctor ordered for a country, and a world, in mourning for the dead President. Released that summer, the movie was a huge and immediate hit. "It worked for American audiences and was an international success as well," Paul said. "We'd get letters saying, 'I've seen *A Hard Day's Night* 75 times, and I love it!'" In a pre-Internet world, the movie lifted the Beatles to a level of global fame never seen before: they were Elvis times four.

The group toured internationally in June and July, then returned to the U.S. in August for a 23-city concert swing that began at San Francisco's Cow Palace, a huge auditorium capable of seating over 10,000. All the venues on the tour were equally large, an accommodation to the Beatles' new mega-popularity. It simply no longer made sense—financially, at any rate—for their handlers to book them into a conventional theater. But with success came unanticipated challenges.

"Something strange had happened in America since their first visit," writes Howard Sounes. "The Beatles were now not only screamed at by their fans but a focus for nut cases and extremists. BEATLE WORSHIP IS IDOLATRY read a placard wielded by a picket of the ultra-

Beatlemania arrives in America, clockwise from top left: The singers alight in New York City, on Feb. 7, 1964, and thousands of fans greet them at the airport; the band makes its second appearance on *The Ed Sullivan Show* just a week after its first; overjoyed fans gather outside the Plaza Hotel; when the movie version opens in August, the mania is in full swing.

religious at the San Francisco show." The frenzy for the band seemed of a different order in America than elsewhere, and frenzy could lead to bad places. In the wake of the JFK assassination, Paul, in particular, was haunted by the fear that a lone assassin with a rifle might single him out.

And then there were the shows. The screaming, too, had risen to new levels. Bill Medley of the Righteous Brothers, who opened for the Beatles, told Bob Spitz that he felt "terrible" for them. "They were real players and singers, doing songs they'd written themselves, and yet they weren't being heard beyond the first or second row. I remember standing by the stage and thinking: 'This can't be any fun for them.'"

During a photo shoot for LIFE magazine, on their first U.S. visit, the Beatles are persuaded to take a dip in a Miami pool.

PAUL TURNED 22 ON TOUR, and he was approaching his physical zenith. The press had already dubbed him the "Cute Beatle," but now, as the baby fat faded, his face, with its soulful eyes and long lashes, took on a melting, masculine beauty that made his female fans—especially those lucky enough to meet him—swoon.

Peggy Lipton, a young Hollywood actress who would later gain some brief fame as a star on TV's *Mod Squad,* was one of those fans. She was just 17 when she met McCartney at a summer garden party in Bel Air. She'd been obsessed with him from the moment she first became aware of the Beatles. Her knees buckled when she shook hands with him, she wrote in her autobiography: "I was madly in love with Paul McCartney, or should I say even more madly in love—knowing full well that disaster lay ahead. How could it be otherwise? Every woman wanted Paul."

And she got him, that night and the next, two nights of mad passion that both lived up to all her dreams—"Paul was a romantic. A confirmation of how I had pictured him for the last year"—and ultimately left her feeling used: "He left town as the tour moved on."

But that was the way of the road, and those were the rules of the game. Many years later, Paul told his biographer Barry Miles that he kept his own set of rules in those days: "I had a girlfriend, and I would go with other girls. It was a perfectly open relationship." Whether Jane Asher felt the same was another question.

THAT AUGUST, THE TOUR BROUGHT the Beatles back to New York, where they played Forest Hills Tennis Stadium. And one night, an acquaintance of John's, a rock journalist named Al Aronowitz, came to visit the group in its hotel suite with a friend of his, Bob Dylan. The young singer-songwriter had been electrifying young audiences on both sides of the Atlantic with his dazzlingly poetic, deeply personal, folk-tinged music, and the Beatles were thrilled to meet him. "He was our idol," Paul said.

It was an exciting meeting all around. Dylan in turn was fascinated by the Beatles—not just as songwriters but as a show-business phenomenon. Each possessed something the other wanted: Dylan had poetic integrity, the Beatles, chart-busting success.

The American also had something else when he came to the Beatles' hotel suite that night: marijuana. The Beatles had tried it, but they'd never had anything as strong as the grass Dylan brought. "We had a crazy party," Paul recalled. "I went around thinking I'd found the meaning of life that night." Accordingly, he wrote it down on a piece of paper. When he looked at the scrap of paper the next day, it read as follows: "There are seven levels."

The meaning of life may not have been discovered that night, but the meeting would have important repercussions for all five artists. Dylan would soon find a way to put rock 'n' roll into his music, and the Beatles would find a way to put introspective poetry into theirs. "We got more and more free to get into ourselves," Paul said. "Our student selves, rather than 'we must please the girls and make money.'"

Getting into themselves would also mean getting ever more deeply into drugs.

EARLY IN 1965, the Beatles arrived in the Bahamas to begin shooting their second movie, *Help!*, once again with director Richard Lester. Brian Epstein traveled with the group, stayed long enough to assure himself that all was in order, then said goodbye to his prize clients and returned to England. "No doubt about it, I thought," he wrote in a diary entry, "they're enjoying making this film very much, relaxed, inventive and effervescent as ever."

In fact, while they may have been relaxed and effervescent, mainly they were stoned. "We were smoking marijuana for breakfast," John Lennon said. "Nobody could communicate with us; it was all glazed eyes and giggling all the time. In our own world."

The wheel had turned mightily since *A Hard Day's Night.* That movie, shot in a black and white that befitted the drabness of England in the not-yet-swinging '60s, showed the birth of the Beatles, the joyous phenomenon that would put an end to all drabness. No four people had ever had such fun just by being themselves. They were total naturals, and the world loved them for it. *Help!*, shot in bright color, was a cartoon movie, a James Bond spoof: the Beatles were now playing themselves rather than being themselves. "While we'd really tried to get involved and learn the script for *A Hard Day's Night,*" Paul recalled, "by the time *Help!* came along, we were taking it as a bit of a joke."

Were they still naturals? Not in this movie, for all its giddy charms. In a very real way, the Beatles had become caricatures. The world still loved them, but it loved them too much, and they were retreating inward. The best part of *Help!* was the sound track. The Beatles could still give the world their music—great music, more personal and complicated every week—but Paul, John, George and Ritchie had decided to keep their selves to themselves.

CHAPTER 3

Getting Better All the Time

AS THE STORY GOES, PAUL MCCARTNEY dreamed the song one night in late 1963, in his attic bedroom at the Ashers' house on Wimpole Street. "I just fell out of bed, found out what key I had dreamed it in, and it seemed near G, and I played it," he recalled. The chords simply fell into place on the piano, so perfectly that Paul thought he was remembering a jazz ballad he'd heard somewhere, maybe one of the old standards his dad, Jim, used to play after dinner on the family upright. For the next month, he plagued friends and acquaintances with the tune: What was it? Did anybody know it?

In 1965, when Paul is just 23, he and the Beatles make one of the greatest albums rock has ever produced. "*Rubber Soul* broke everything open," said Steve Winwood.

Nobody did. "Eventually it became like handing something in to the police," McCartney said. "I thought if no one claimed it after a few weeks, then I could have it."

No one claimed it because it was all his. The song was "Yesterday"—although the title and words wouldn't come to Paul for more than a year. For a long time, the working title of the haunting melody was "Scrambled Eggs." The dummy lyrics began: "Scrambled eggs/ Oh my baby how I love your legs."

Oh, baby. The mid-'60s were a sexy time for Paul McCartney. Still in his early 20s, he was at the height of his powers, creatively, physically and financially: a young genius getting richer and more famous every day, the fantasy of millions of women, he strode the world like a sun king. And nowhere was his dominion more satisfying than in his adopted home of London, where in one great surge, the boy who only yesterday had been a nobody from the north had ascended the Himalayas of snobbery in one of the most socially stratified cities on earth. "There was a wide-eyed fascination as once-closed doors were flung open to him," Bob Spitz writes. "'Right this way, Mr. McCartney.' 'Our best table, Mr. McCartney.' 'It's on the house, Mr. McCartney.'

The new rock royalty, clockwise from left: Fans behold their icon at a Milan concert in 1965; McCartney and his girlfriend of five years, Jane Asher, attend the 1967 London premiere of *How I Won the War,* in which Lennon plays a role; Princess Margaret meets the Beatles at the 1965 premiere of their second film, *Help!*; Paul chats with TV host David Frost at a 1965 music-awards lunch. Paul tended to enjoy the limelight and live concerts more than his bandmates did.

Mr. McCartney! He could barely contain his joy over the classy ring to it."

Class meant everything to Paul, according to Spitz. "Respect was class; fine art was class; French dining was class. Social status especially provided class, which he solicited in earnest through his ties to the Ashers."

Yet even as he cherished those ties, he was breaking free. In 1965, his accountant informed him that he was a millionaire. "He was earning so much, he kept fat envelopes of spare cash in his sock drawer at Wimpole Street," Howard Sounes writes. "He'd done the right thing by his nearest and dearest, buying Dad a house ... and giving his kid brother an allowance; he'd treated himself to some boys' toys, notably his Aston Martin and Radford Mini de Ville (a souped-up Mini with a luxurious interior); and he'd given Jane some nice gifts, too, bits of jewelry and other fripperies. Now he proved how serious he was about their relationship by taking Jane shopping for a house."

The place he chose was a big brick Regency on Cavendish Avenue, a sedate street in the posh neighborhood of St. John's Wood, just a short walk from Regent's Park and the EMI studios on

Abbey Road. A proper dwelling for a young English gentleman of wealth and taste—and still McCartney's London home today.

Yet even as he lived under the Ashers' roof and went house shopping with their elder daughter, he was asserting his sun-king privileges. Apparently his open relationship with Jane was in force while he was not only on the road but also in London. "Living in the Asher house gave me the base and the freedom and the independence," Paul told his friend and biographer Barry Miles. "I was pretty free."

Asher kept her feelings about the arrangement to herself. The one intimate of Paul's who didn't was John Lennon. "I remember John very much envying me," Paul recalled. "He said, 'Well, if you go out with another girl, what does Jane think?' And I said, 'Well, I don't care what she thinks—we're not married. We've got a perfectly sensible relationship.' He was jealous of that because at this time, he couldn't do that. He was married to Cynthia and with a lot of energy bursting to get out. He'd tried to give Cynthia the traditional thing, but you kind of knew he couldn't. There were cracks appearing, but he could only paste them over by staying at home and getting very wrecked."

While Paul was riding high, John was miserable: he meant the theme song he wrote for *Help!* quite literally. "The whole Beatle thing was just beyond comprehension," he said. "I was eating and drinking like a pig, and I was fat as a pig, dissatisfied with myself, and subconsciously, I was crying for help. It was my fat Elvis period."

Lennon's discontent thrust him along a path of self-exploration. The Beatles' meeting with Bob Dylan the previous August and the marijuana they'd smoked together were major catalysts. "You've Got to Hide Your Love Away," another Lennon song on the *Help!* sound track, played as though Dylan himself could have written it. Love was still the subject, but just barely. John wanted to go further still. All four of them did. In May, the Beatles sneaked into a Dylan performance at the Royal Albert Hall and were awestruck by the singer-songwriter's ability—still with just his scratchy voice and an acoustic guitar, at that point—to rivet a huge audience with the emotional intensity of his poetic imagination.

Not long afterward, John and George, along with Cynthia Lennon and George's girlfriend Pattie Boyd, went to a dinner party at the home of a friend, a London dentist with a swinging reputation. After dinner, the two Beatles and the women drank some coffee, which, the dentist revealed to John, had been laced with LSD.

John and his wife Cynthia beam with anticipation of the Beatles' first flight to New York in 1964, but by the time he appears with Paul on a TV show in 1965, right, he is feeling cooped up in his domestic life.

Few people had heard of the drug at that time; Lennon and Harrison barely knew what it was. But soon they and the two women were tripping, nightclubbing through a London that had been transformed into an exhilarating, terrifying phantasmagoria. "It was insane, going around London on it," John recalled. "We thought when we went to the club that it was on fire, and then we thought there was a premiere, and it was just an ordinary light outside."

"Suddenly I felt the most incredible feeling come over me," George remembered. "It was

As the band enters a surreal phase, in 1965, Paul enjoys the mind-opening effects of marijuana, but for a time, he is the lone Beatles holdout when it comes to dropping LSD.

something like a very concentrated version of the best feeling I'd ever had in my whole life ... I felt in love, not with anything or anybody in particular but with everything ... Then suddenly, it felt as if a bomb had made a direct hit on the nightclub, and the roof had been blown off."

"The boys couldn't wait to tell Paul," Howard Sounes writes. "John had always loved *Alice in Wonderland,* and here was a drug that could send him down the rabbit hole any time he liked. He urged Paul to take LSD without delay."

Paul demurred. "When acid came 'round, we'd heard that ... it alters your life and you never think the same again, and I think John was rather excited by that prospect," he said. "I was rather frightened by that prospect. I thought, 'Just what I need! Some funny little thing where I can never get back home again.'"

Paul was quite at home with himself and perfectly happy with the way he thought, thank you very much. In late May, while he was on a vacation in Portugal with Jane, the words to "Yesterday" finally came to him, all in a rush. The melancholy and unresolved lyric about lost love was a striking one for such a blazingly successful young man to have written: in matters of the heart, Paul had always seemed to be the one in control. Listening to the words today, though—"Why she had to go/ I don't know, she wouldn't say"—it's hard not to think of the one anguish he never liked to talk about, the sudden and unexplained loss of his mother in October 1956. At the time, the 14-year-old Paul wasn't even told the cause of her death.

Back in London in June, he recorded the song solo, the first time any Beatle had ever laid down a track without the others (George Martin later overdubbed a string-quartet accompaniment). Martin felt that the song should rightfully be credited to McCartney alone, but Brian Epstein was adamantly opposed. "No, whatever we do, we are not splitting up the Beatles," the manager said.

But the wedge had been inserted. "Yesterday," which would go on to become one of the most covered songs of all time, was released later that summer and quickly shot to No. 1 in the U.S. Four of the five prior Beatles No. 1's had been songs chiefly written by Lennon; after "Yesterday," six of the next seven of the group's top-selling singles were composed solely or mainly by McCartney. The group's leadership had shifted. More and more, though, they were a group of individuals.

THE BEATLES' RETURN TO THE U.S. in August 1965 brought the singers to a very different country than the one they'd left just a year before. The '60s were in full swing, a new world had opened up, and rock 'n' roll was at the center of it. The Fab Four had uncorked the bottle; the whirlwind swirled. The Rolling Stones, the Who, the Animals, the Kinks and the Zombies, among other groups, had joined the British Invasion. Bob Dylan had come right back at them, going electric at the Newport Folk Festival that summer. And though his fans were duly outraged, an American rock revolution was under way. The Beatles, as torchbearers of a generation, would have to respond in kind. They were up to the task.

But first, a lot of strange territory had to be covered. There was their North American tour, for one thing: all arenas this time around. No rock group had ever done it before. It all began with the legendary Aug. 15 Shea Stadium concert: 30 minutes of Beatles music, virtually none of it audible amid the jet-engine shriek generated by 55,600 fans in attendance. Mick Jagger, sitting near the field with Keith Richards, was unsettled. "It's frightening," he said. Paul didn't mind a bit. "Once you go onstage, and you know you've filled a place that size, it's magic; just walls of people," he said. "I don't think we were heard much by the audience ... We just did our thing, cheap and cheerful, ran to a waiting limo and sped off."

The Beatles met the same scene at every stadium and coliseum they played as they swung westward: Toronto, Atlanta, Houston—once more winding up on the West Coast, where they hit Portland, San Diego, Los Angeles and San Francisco, with a few days' R&R in L.A. in between.

The bandmates rented a big, horseshoe-shaped house in the Hollywood Hills, and the scene was surreal, with fans laying siege—some girls rented a helicopter and buzzed the place—and John and George tripping on LSD and trying to get the others to join in. "John and I had decided

After Beatlemania strikes, the live-concert career of the Beatles does not last long. Their legendary Shea Stadium concert, in August 1965, above, is 30 minutes of music, drowned out by shrieking so intense that concertgoer Mick Jagger calls it "frightening." Just a year later, they give a half-hearted concert at San Francisco's Candlestick Park, below right, that proves to be their last big public performance.

that Paul and Ringo had to have acid because we couldn't relate to them anymore," George recalled. "Not just on the one level—we couldn't relate to them on any level because acid had changed us so much."

Ringo took the drug; Paul, once again, held off. "Paul felt very out of it," John said, "because we are all slightly cruel: 'We're all taking it, and you're not.' It was a long time before Paul took it."

Perhaps even more surreal, though, was the group's visit to Elvis Presley. A meeting between rock's chief deities, the old guard and the new, had been under negotiation for months; finally, Brian Epstein and Colonel Tom Parker worked it out. The Beatles were beside themselves with nerves. Elvis' "Heartbreak Hotel"—beamed in to Liverpool on the staticky signal of Radio Luxembourg—was what had turned them all into rockers. Elvis wasn't just their idol; he was a god.

The Beatles meet Elvis, in 1965, at his mansion in Bel Air, Calif., where they had a jam session in the living room. "He was our greatest idol," said Paul, "but the styles were changing in favor of us."

The King had a mansion in Bel Air, just across the hills; the Beatles traveled there in a limo, smoking so much pot on the way that by the time they arrived, "we were all in hysterics," George Harrison recalled.

Their giggles turned to awe when they walked through the home's circular foyer and into the pleasure dome that was the living room. There, amid a pool table, jukebox, bar and a gaggle of hangers-on, Elvis Presley himself sat on a couch, plucking on an electric bass and watching TV with the sound off. The Beatles gaped. "I mean, it was Elvis," Paul remembered. "He just looked like Elvis."

The hangers-on greeted the Beatles' party. "We went in—he had a crowd of guys with him," Ringo said recently. "It was a little awkward." The guys were the so-called Memphis Mafia, Elvis' retinue, who, "with their women, were swarming all around us with noisy greets and large drinks," Beatles PR man Tony Barrow, who was also there that night—and who'd been ordered to make sure no writers or photographers would be present—told TIME. "But beneath all this superficial hospitality, the five superstars at the center of the whole shindig had precious little to say to each other. Their conversation was stilted and artificially friendly."

Until it shifted to a common language. There were guitars and a piano in the living room, and within minutes, an informal jam session had begun: a couple of Elvis' hits, a couple of the Beatles' hits—Barrow remembered "I Feel Fine" being played. After a couple of drinks, Paul found his confidence—and common ground in the instrument the King was playing: "That was the great thing for me—that he was into the bass," he remembered. "So there I was: 'Well, let me show you a thing or two, El.' ... Suddenly, he was a mate."

None of the other three, for all their pleasant memories of that very strange evening, presumed to get so close.

"It was one of the great meetings of my life," Paul recalled. "I think he liked us. I think at that time he may have felt a little bit threatened, but he didn't say anything ... I only met him that once, and then I think the success of our career started to push him out a little, which we were very sad about ... He was our greatest idol, but the styles were changing in favor of us."

ELVIS WAS THE PAST, and the Beatles were the present—but only if they stayed ahead of the pack that was pressing in behind them. McCartney and Lennon were up to the challenge. As Paul put it, "We'd had our cute period, and now it was time to expand ... Now we can branch out into songs that are more surreal."

The group's songwriters-in-chief came at surrealism from different angles. Hallucinogenics would ultimately be more meaningful to John than to Paul. LSD had opened new portals of awareness for Lennon and for Harrison, who had discovered Indian music during the making of *Help!* and found himself increasingly interested in the sitar, both as an accompanying instrument and, potentially, as a tool for composition. Marijuana was now central to the lives of all four Beatles.

But it wasn't just about drugs. They were four restless and ambitious young men, with strong appetites for exploration of all kinds and the means to explore. The American tour had been very profitable but artistically deadening; meanwhile, they were maturing as men and blossoming creatively. All at once, the recording studio felt far more congenial than the screaming stadiums. The group came to Abbey Road in the fall of 1965 with a new assurance: "We were getting better, technically and musically," John said. "We finally took over the studio"—pointedly meaning that this was the moment George Martin changed from a studio boss to a more reserved and well-groomed member of the group.

Lennon and McCartney had undergone a quantum leap as composers, both lyrically—"Dylan was influencing us quite heavily at that point," Paul said—and musically. "They were ready for new ... directions," Martin said. "Other influences became apparent: classical influences and modern music."

The result was, quite simply, an epochal album, to this day one of the greatest rock has ever produced. "*Rubber Soul* broke everything open," Steve Winwood told Bob Spitz. "It crossed music into a whole new dimension and was responsible for kicking off the '60s rock era as we know it."

Again, love was a formidable and central subject ("the underlying theme to the universe," in John's words), but suddenly the Beatles were finding new and more sophisticated ways to explore the theme—witness John's "Norwegian Wood" (accompanied

When Bob Dylan goes electric at Newport, in 1965, an American rock revolution is under way. The Beatles will have to respond in kind.

by George's sitar) and Paul's "Michelle"—and even moving entirely beyond it. "In My Life"—a composition so strong that both Paul and John would later claim authorship—is a towering achievement: on the surface, just a wistful reminiscence of lost times but—with its simple, deeply affecting lyrics, its haunting tune and tight harmonies—also one of the great poetic achievements of the English language. That the Beatles were capable of this not much more than a year after "She Loves You" and "I'm Happy Just to Dance With You" is astonishing.

Paul McCartney was very aware of how far he'd come. Another song on *Rubber Soul,* his seemingly cheerful and bouncy "I'm Looking Through You," reflects a marked change in his relationship with Jane Asher:

Rubber Soul, **recorded at Abbey Road studios in 1965, is a towering achievement. Says Paul: "We'd had our cute period, and now it was time to expand."**

> *You're thinking of me the same old way,*
> *You were above me, but not today*

McCartney's creative and commercial ambitions, driven by a growing awareness of his formidable musical powers, were enormous. He was capable of great fun, but no matter how hard he played, he saw his goals clearly at all times. He looked like a cherub, and he could charm the birds out of the trees—until he was crossed, thwarted or challenged. "Paul can be very cynical and much more biting than me, when he's driven to it," John Lennon said. "Of course, he's got more patience, but he can carve people up in no time at all when he's pushed. He hits the nail right on the head and doesn't beat about the bush, does Paul."

WHERE DRUGS HARDER THAN POT were concerned, Paul McCartney was a latecomer and a skeptic. Until 1966, he was the Beatles' lone LSD holdout, and when he finally took the drug, he didn't like it.

A friend, a young aristrocrat named Tara Browne—soon to be killed in a car wreck that John would immortalize in "A Day in the Life"—offered Paul acid after a night at a London club. "Paul's first trip wasn't pleasant," Sounes writes. "He became overly conscious of how dirty his shirt was and felt too exhausted the next day to do any work."

But if LSD brought out the prissy workaholic in Paul, cannabis was another matter. That spring he wrote a giddily upbeat love song that would be featured on the new Beatles album *Revolver.* The song was "Got to Get You Into My Life," and as Paul freely admitted to biographer Barry Miles, it wasn't about a girl at all; it was about marijuana.

"I'd been a rather straight, working-class lad, but when we started to get into pot, it seemed to me to be quite uplifting," he said. "It didn't seem to have too many side effects like alcohol or some of the other stuff like pills, which I pretty much kept off ... I didn't have a hard time with it, and to me, it was mind expanding, literally mind expanding."

More and more, the mind—and by extension, the recording studio—was becoming the Beatles' theater, the place where they could be playful and experimental at a safe remove from the world's grasping. "It's as if we were painters who had never really been allowed to paint—

we'd just had to go selling our paintings up and down the country," said Paul. "Then suddenly we had somebody telling us, 'You can have a studio, and you can paint, and you can take your time.' So, obviously, being in a recording studio became much more attractive to us than going on the road again."

Still, of the four Beatles, McCartney was the most deeply committed to show business and the one who minded touring least. "We were getting fed up with that aspect," he said, "but I think I could have handled it. I expect that when you become famous."

And off they went again. Yet two passages in 1966 brought the unpleasantness of touring to a head. In July, in the Philippines, the group caused riots after unintentionally offending First Lady Imelda Marcos: Brian Epstein had turned down an invitation for the group to attend a reception at the presidential palace. The Beatles made a narrow escape from the airport through a menacing gauntlet of soldiers and police. They were never paid for their concert.

In August, they returned once more to the U.S., only to find themselves in the midst of a bitter controversy. In March, John had given an interview in which he'd taken a characteristically sardonic view of the Beatles' place in the world: "We're more popular than Jesus now," he said. "I don't know which will go first, rock 'n' roll or Christianity."

That did not go down well in America, to say the least: right-wing and religious groups mounted anti-Beatles demonstrations and burned the group's records. The tour was marred by protests and press conferences in which John was constantly urged to apologize for remarks he felt had been taken out of context. There were death threats, particularly in Memphis: at a concert, somebody set off a firecracker while the band was onstage. All the Beatles looked at one another with the same thought: one of them had been shot.

"George and John were the ones most against touring; they got particularly fed up," Paul recalled. "I'd been trying to say, 'Ah, touring's good, and it keeps us sharp … musicians need to play. Keep music live.' I had held on to that attitude when there were doubts, but finally I agreed with them."

On Monday, Aug. 29, 1966, a cool, windswept night in San Francisco, the Beatles played to a half-filled stadium of 25,000 fans at Candlestick Park. It was a half-hearted concert, too—the same 11 songs, the same stilted patter, in and out in 30 minutes. And when the four ran off the field to a waiting armored car, they all knew the same thing: after almost 1,300 concerts, this, amazingly, was their last. Beatlemania was over.

"*RUBBER SOUL* WAS the pot album, and *Revolver* was the acid," John Lennon said, and though he was mainly speaking autobiographically—as Lennon was mainly wont to speak—he was expressing a fundamental truth about each album's essence. But whatever trips John, George and Ringo were taking, Paul was the one who made *Revolver* psychedelic by sheer force of artistic and intellectual will. "I'm trying to cram everything in, all the things that I've missed," he said at the time. "People are saying things and painting things and writing things and composing things that are great, and I must know what people are doing. I vaguely mind people knowing anything I don't know."

"The depth of Paul's musical genius is something that became clear gradually and, at the same time, the depth of his musical curiosity and his ability to learn things fast," Peter Asher recalled. "Not just any instrument he picked up but any kind of music that came his way." So while John explored his interior landscape, Paul investigated the outer world. It was his interest in backward tape-recorder effects and the avant-garde music of composers like John Cage and Karlheinz Stockhausen that made *Revolver* sound utterly different from any other pop album

At their peak, the Beatles are prolific. While recording their breakthrough 1966 album *Revolver*, at Abbey Road, they also produce a single, "Paperback Writer" (backed with "Rain"), which becomes a No. 1 hit.

George's immersion in Indian music and mysticism emerges
in sitar-driven moments on the *Revolver* album. Here, he plays
for girlfriend Pattie Boyd.

ever. Lennon may have come up with the mystical-chemical lyrics to the last track, "Tomorrow Never Knows"—"Turn off your mind, relax and float downstream"—as well as the idea of a song that would drone along in one key; George's backup tambura was richly atmospheric, and Ringo's propulsive drumming dazzling; but it was Paul's wild tape-loop sounds that made the number mind-bending.

The album was a shimmering bouquet of brilliancies—inner meditations, love songs, whimsies—made by a group in the process of becoming individuals. George, who was beginning to steep himself in Indian music and mysticism, showed with "Taxman" and the sitar- and tabla-driven "Love You To" that he was starting to come into his own as a composer. But Paul's "Eleanor Rigby," a literary contemplation of loneliness gorgeously driven by a classical string quartet (George Martin's idea), was in a category by itself. If he wasn't inclined to be introspective, he was capable of creating unforgettable characters.

Driven by Paul's avant-garde instincts, the bandmates spend six months in 1967 recording *Sgt. Pepper*. Says producer George Martin: "They wanted every trick brought out of the bag."

AFTER THE LAST CONCERT, the Beatles went their separate ways for a bit, taking a longed-for break from the grind of tour-album-tour. George, who'd been jolted into a spiritual awakening by LSD, traveled to India to study sitar with Ravi Shankar; John, with Ringo along for company, headed to Spain to play a small role in a Richard Lester film, *How I Won the War*. Meanwhile, with Jane acting in a Shakespeare play, Paul went off on an exploration of his own: a solo motor trip in France, disguised in fake chin whiskers and mustache. But in Bordeaux, the disguise worked too well: he was refused admission to a discotheque, the kind of snub that fame had allowed him to forget about. "So I thought, 'Sod this, I might as well go back to the hotel and come as him!'" he told Barry Miles. "So I came back as a normal Beatle and was welcomed with open arms."

A narrow escape from anonymity. Still, the episode got him thinking about identities. Now that touring was over, now that the Beatles were no longer to be identically dressed, adorable mop-tops who mimed playing their instruments under the white noise of screaming crowds, who were they to be as a band? How could the Beatles be reinvented?

Flying back from Africa, where Jane had met him for a photo safari, he mused on the question while toying with the salt and pepper packets on his seat-back tray. Then he took a second look at the pepper, and an idea began to form.

"It was at the start of the hippie times, and there was a jingly-jangly hippie aura all around in America," Paul recalled. "I started thinking about what would be a really mad name to call a band. At the time there were lots of groups with names like 'Laughing Joe and His Medicine Band' ... all that old western going-round-on-wagons stuff, with long rambling names. And so ... I threw those words together: 'Sgt. Pepper's Lonely Hearts Club Band.'"

THE IDEA WAS TO CREATE a fictional band, a kind of group disguise the Beatles could wear, removing with one wave of a magic wand the constant pressure of being Beatles. Paul was enthusiastic, the others less so. The months away from making music had taken them all to strange places. John in particular was lost: lying around his suburban mansion stoned, unshaven; staring at the TV; paying little attention to Cynthia or their 3-year-old son, Julian; and now and then picking up a guitar and singing a scrap of a tune he'd been toying with for weeks: "Living is easy with eyes closed …"

But then a chance meeting pointed him in another direction. A friend who ran an avant-garde London gallery invited Lennon to a preview of a show by a new conceptual artist every-one was talking about. John went reluctantly and at first stared skeptically at the odd objects on display: "All sorts of contraptions, connected by gangplanks, beams and ladders," according to Bob Spitz. But then the gallery owner introduced Lennon to the artist, "a slip of a young Asian

Paul's idea for *Sgt. Pepper* is to create a fictional band, a kind of group disguise. He is the primary writer of eight of the album's 13 songs.

woman … prim, in a black leotard and pale as porridge." Her name was Yoko Ono.

In the meantime, rock 'n' roll was busily moving into the vacuum left by the inactive Fab Four: both Eric Clapton's super-group, Cream, and a sizzling new guitarist named Jimi Hendrix were making big noise all over Britain. The Beach Boys had recently been voted the world's best vocal group in a U.K. music poll. It was galling. "I think we were itching to get going," Paul said. But at this point, there was only one place to go: EMI's Studio Two at Abbey Road. The problem was that John and Paul hadn't written to-gether in months.

Yet when Lennon sat in front of George Martin and strummed the tune he'd been working on, Martin was thunderstruck. "I was spellbound," he recalled. "I was in love … He had broken through into different territory, to a place I did not recognize from his past songs … It was dreamlike without being fey, weird without being pretentious." The song was "Strawberry Fields Forever."

The Beatles spent the next month working on John's unprecedented piece of musical poetry, which distilled—through the lens of LSD consciousness—all the pain of growing up angry and confused at his Aunt Mimi's house in suburban Liverpool, his mother nearby but out of reach and then, in one terrible instant, gone forever. As a boy, he'd crossed the road behind Mimi's backyard and sneaked over a wall to play and dream on the wooded grounds of an orphanage there, Strawberry Field.

The result was a masterpiece. Characteristically undaunted, Paul responded with a master-piece of his own. Also characteristically, he tapped nostalgia rather than pain in his reminiscence of a Liverpool boyhood. Like "Strawberry Fields," "Penny Lane" paints a picture with images, yet McCartney's is a different kind of poetry: cheerful-wistful rather than world-weary; photore-alistic rather than hallucinatory; but—as befitted one whose drug of choice was pot rather than acid—slightly surreal in its clarity. The fireman with his hourglass, the pretty nurse selling poppies, the blue suburban skies: you see them in your mind's eye but feel them as much as see them.

Lennon and McCartney had entered a new realm in songwriting. But they had entered it separately.

"STRAWBERRY FIELDS FOREVER" and "Penny Lane" were supposed to go onto the album that became *Sgt. Pepper's Lonely Hearts Club Band,* but it didn't work out that way. Instead, they came out as a rare, double-A-sided single in February 1967—one of the most brilliant singles of all time but unfortunately distinguished as the first Beatles single not to hit No. 1 in the U.K., after 12 chart toppers in a row. "Strawberry"/"Penny" was blocked from the top by Engelbert Humperdinck's "Release Me," which it actually outsold—except John and Paul's two A-sides got counted, all too symbolically, as two separate singles. And if "Release Me" wasn't in the same artistic realm as John and Paul's disc, it had the virtue, at least as far as the general record-buying public was concerned, of being easily understandable. Even some critics were baffled at first by the Beatles' single. Derek Johnson, of the U.K.'s *New Musical Express,* wrote, "Quite honestly, I don't know what to make of it."

But many listeners, both amateur and professional, were ecstatic about the new sounds. "[T]he Beatles have developed into the single most creative force in pop music," TIME magazine wrote. "They have bridged the heretofore impassable gap between rock and classical … to achieve the most compellingly original sounds ever heard in pop music."

And this was only the beginning.

ONE NIGHT IN EARLY SPRING, in the midst of the recording sessions for *Sgt. Pepper,* John rummaged in his pill container for some amphetamines and, by mistake, took a tab of LSD. The Beatles occasionally smoked pot while recording and now and then did cocaine, but all knew that acid was likely to derail the serious business—and it was serious, no matter how playful—of making their music in the studio. John's trip, which made him feel ill and paranoid, derailed the process that night, and Paul wound up walking his partner back to the Cavendish Avenue house to help him come down.

It was then Paul decided that the time had come for him to take LSD with John. "I thought … 'It's been coming for a long time,'" he told Barry Miles. "John's on it already, so I'll sort of catch up."

They stayed up all night, a night McCartney would never forget. "[W]e looked into each other's eyes, the eye contact thing we used to do, which is fairly mind-boggling. You dissolve into each other … And it was amazing. You're looking into each other's eyes, and you would want to look away, but you wouldn't, and you could see yourself in the other person. It was a very freaky experience, and I was totally blown away."

Paul had a "big vision" of John that night: he was "a king, the absolute Emperor of Eternity … I could feel every inch of the house, and John seemed like some sort of emperor in control of it all."

And this was Paul's house.

HE FIRST MET HER at a London nightclub in May 1967; then he saw her again four days later at the launch party for *Sgt. Pepper,* at Brian Epstein's London town house. The two meetings weren't coincidental: Linda Eastman was homing in. One of the few women, and few Americans, present at the launch, she was there to photograph the Beatles, but she was really only interested in one of them.

Eastman, the daughter of a wealthy New York entertainment lawyer, was tall and blond and

Future soul mates: In 1967, Paul meets Linda Eastman, first
at a London nightclub and four days later at the launch party,
above, for *Sgt. Pepper* at Brian Epstein's town house.

elegant, brimming with the kind of confidence that good looks and a childhood of privilege can
bestow. Finding herself in a tight spot in her early 20s—divorced and the mother of a young
daughter—she simply decided to reinvent herself as a photographer of rock-'n'-roll stars. "She
seemed ambitious," Peter Asher recalled. "With photographers, it's hard to separate their social
ambitions from their photographic ambitions because they obviously want to meet cool people
and take pictures of them. I think she wanted to do both. She seemed like someone who, when
she decided what she wanted, would go and get it—which works as a photographer and as a
social animal."

Armed with not much more than an expensive camera, her winsome appearance and a brass-
bound self-assurance, Linda had taken pictures of some of the biggest rockers—the Stones and
Dylan and Hendrix, among others—and had been involved with many of them. But the Beatles
were in their own category, and Linda Eastman was looking for more than an involvement.
"She always insisted that she was going to marry Paul McCartney, even before she met him,"
an old family friend recalled.

After a while, Paul would come to think it was a pretty good idea too.

IT TOOK THE BEATLES some six months to record *Sgt. Pepper*—in contrast
to, say, the one day it took them to make their first album, *Please Please Me*—because they wanted
to make the record different from anything they, or anybody else, had ever done. "They wanted
every trick brought out of the bag," George Martin said. Recording engineer Geoff Emerick
recalled, "We had microphones right down in the bells of brass instruments and headphones

turned into microphones attached to violins … [W]e used giant primitive oscillators to vary the speed of instruments and vocals, and we had tapes chopped to pieces and stuck together upside down and the wrong way around."

It was all thrilling—for those who were thrilled by it. As the Beatles' avant-gardist in chief, Paul was the main proponent of technological tricks and, in general, the most hands-on. John, Martin recalled, "would deal in moods … in colors almost, and he would never be specific about what instruments or what line I had … Paul, however, would actually sit down at the piano with me, and we'd work things out."

Meanwhile, Ringo spent a lot of time waiting around to record his percussion parts—"It's a fine album," he said, "but I did learn to play chess while we were recording it"—and George was increasingly disaffected. "Up to that time, we had recorded more like a band," he said. *Sgt. Pepper,* however, "became an assembly process—just little parts and then overdubbing—and for me, it became a bit tiring and a bit boring."

Paul, on the other hand, was more excited than ever. In many ways, *Sgt. Pepper,* from initial concept to final product, was his album: he was the primary writer of eight of its 13 songs (including "When I'm Sixty-Four," which he'd first composed—without lyrics—as a teenager back on Forthlin Road). John wrote just four, although one, "A Day in the Life," was possibly the album's masterpiece, and "Lucy in the Sky With Diamonds," with its coincidental LSD initials, helped give *Sgt. Pepper* its psychedelic reputation. (He also contributed a characteristic phrase to Paul's typically upbeat "It's Getting Better," chiming in after "It's getting better all the time": "It can't get no worse.") Speaking about "Being for the Benefit of Mr. Kite!," a song he wasn't proud of, Lennon later said, "I had to write it quick because otherwise I wouldn't have been on the album." He was exaggerating but pointedly implying that, for better or worse—and for all his Emperor of Eternity status—Paul was now in charge of the Beatles, or whatever the Beatles had become.

"He was always the workaholic," Ringo told Time. "I thanked him that the Beatles made more records than they would've if he hadn't been in the band, because we would just be sitting in the garden—relaxing, let's say. Heh-heh. Phone would ring, and Paul would say, 'Hey, it's time we made another record.' So we'd go in and make music."

Paul was bursting with ideas. One was to make another movie, to be directed and produced by the Beatles, without outside interference from grownups—as they then thought of the business types and other authority figures they were constantly forced to deal with. Paul's concept for the new film, perhaps inspired by a trip he'd recently taken to check out the thriving hippie culture of San Francisco, was as unstructured as the times demanded: the Beatles would simply ride around the English countryside on a tour bus with friends and acquaintances, filming themselves having adventures, whatever the adventures might be. A Magical Mystery Tour. The problem being that everything seemed magical and mysterious when you were stoned, considerably less so when you looked at it afterward.

BUT THE NEXT BIG IDEA was George's. It came like a cymbal crash: he

was giving up LSD. "It enables you to see a lot of possibilities that you may never have noticed before, but it isn't the answer," he said. The answer, he thought, was God.

His spiritual awakening had begun when he'd traveled to India to study sitar with Ravi Shankar. When he returned, he gave books about Hinduism to Paul, John and Ringo. Then they heard Maharishi Mahesh Yogi was coming to England.

"We'd seen him years before on a Granada TV current-affairs program," Paul recalled.

"There he was, just a giggling little swami who was going around the world to promote peace. So when … somebody said there was a meeting, we all went, 'Oh, that's that giggly little guy. We've seen him. He's great.'

"I think there was a little bit of emptiness in our souls, a lack of spiritual fulfillment. We were seeing all this stuff on acid … glimpsing bits of bliss, and we wanted to know, and I guess I still do, how best to approach that."

Paul, John and George, along with Jane Asher and Pattie Boyd (now George's wife), went to a lecture by the Maharishi in London, then had a 90-minute audience with him. The guru told the Beatles that there was no creator God; the path to bliss was through meditation. "We liked him," Paul said.

So much so, that all the Beatles, including Ringo, went to Wales in August 1967 to attend a 10-day seminar by the Maharishi and learn how to meditate. The second day they were there, an emergency phone call came through: Brian Epstein had died of a drug overdose.

EPSTEIN, ALWAYS DEEPLY CONFLICTED about his homosexuality, had been particularly depressed lately: his father had recently died, and he was anxious about his relationship with the Beatles. His management contract was to expire at the end of September, and though he knew the boys were going to keep him on, he also knew that his commission was going to be sharply reduced. With the band no longer touring, there was very little left for him to do. He was living in a constant state of gnawing insecurity, addicted to amphetamines, barbiturates and alcohol. His death, caused by some combination of these, was ruled accidental.

All the Beatles grieved heavily for their old friend, the man who had been instrumental in making them stars. "It was shattering, sad and a little frightening," Paul said. "We loved him."

They also felt adrift. In a world of untrustworthy grownups, Brian had been the one who took care of them. John was the most distraught of all. "I didn't really have any misconceptions about our being able to do anything other than play music, and I was scared," he said. "I thought, we've had it now."

Typically, Paul—who had all kinds of ambitions beyond playing music—supplanted fear and sentiment with supreme practicality. "We'd always wanted to get the tools of the art into our own hands," he said later. "Even before we got into our own company, Apple, we were virtually managing ourselves. So Brian had become a bit redundant."

At Epstein's death, the group, with £2 million in the bank that could either be paid in taxes or put into a business, had already taken the first steps toward forming its own company. What, precisely, this company would do, none of the bandmates had quite figured out yet.

THAT FALL, THE BEATLES MADE their movie—or rather, Paul's movie. McCartney both directed and edited *Magical Mystery Tour,* about which the best that could be said is that it was an extended music video before its time, complete with a half-dozen new songs, including the title song, "I Am the Walrus" and "The Fool on the Hill." Populating the hourlong film was a tour bus filled with ordinary-looking working-class men and women having the time of their lives and, amid druggy dream sequences featuring piles of spaghetti and the Beatles wearing animal heads, dozens of extras of every variety: dwarfs; fat people; costumed nuns, vicars and soccer players. The worst that could be said about *Magical Mystery Tour* was that it was a plotless, absurdist mishmash of a road picture, fun for the group to make (and no doubt a kind of exorcism of the pain of Brian's death) and—broadcast by the BBC the day

Paul, with Jane Asher, after hearing about the death by overdose of Beatles manager Brian Epstein, right, says it is "shattering, sad and a little frightening. We loved him."

after Christmas—misery to watch. "Appalling!" said the *Daily Mail.* "Blatant rubbish," said the *Daily Express.*

The music got better reviews. In England, a double EP containing the film's six songs was a hit, and in the U.S., an LP with both the sound track and the Beatles' five 1967 singles (including "Strawberry Fields Forever" and "Penny Lane") was No. 1 for eight weeks, garnering huge sales and rave notices.

Musically speaking, the Beatles seemed to be back on track. All they were missing was a grownup to tell them what to do next.

NOW THAT PAUL WAS 25, starting to settle down seemed the adult thing to do. Accordingly, that Christmas he gave Jane a diamond and emerald ring, and they announced their engagement to their families.

Yet the betrothal was more an attempt at repair than a deeply heartfelt gesture: wide fissures had been forming in the relationship over the past four years. For one thing, Jane had no interest in marijuana or any other drug. But more important, Paul's bond with his bandmates, and especially John, was the central connection in his life. The Beatles had enjoyed bachelorhood to the maximum, and even the arrival of significant females did little to change that. Almost equally problematic for Paul was Jane's very busy acting career. "I always wanted to beat her down," he told biographer Hunter Davies. "I wanted her to give up work completely."

But Jane, gifted in her own right and a strong personality, refused. "I've been brought up to be always doing something," she said. "And I enjoy acting. I didn't want to give that up."

Paul appeared to retreat. "I know now I was just being silly," he told Jane, in front of Davies.

"It was a game, trying to beat you down."

But the game was serious. He couldn't change his own nature—"Jane confided in me enough to say that Paul wanted her to become the little woman at home with the kiddies," Cynthia Lennon later wrote—any more than Jane could change hers. And further games were soon to follow.

THE BEATLES DECIDED to get away from it all—far away. In February, all four, along with the women, traveled to the Maharishi's ashram in Rishikesh, India, by the headwaters of the Ganges, in the Himalayan foothills, for what was planned to be a three-month program of meditation and spiritual education. Donovan, the Beach Boys' Mike Love and Mia Farrow were also present. John and George were eager acolytes; Ringo and Paul, not so much.

Rishikesh was hot and buggy; all the students, no matter how rich or famous, lived in small huts. Ringo and his wife Maureen—who hated the heat, the insects and the food, and missed the two young sons they'd left at home—lasted two weeks. Paul and Jane stayed a little longer. He enjoyed meditating: "That was the most pleasant, the most relaxed I ever got. For a few minutes, I really felt so light, so floating, so complete," he said.

But "the difficulty, of course, is keeping your mind clear," he told Barry Miles. "[B]ecause the minute you clear it, a thought comes in and says, 'What are we gonna do about our next record?'"

In truth, meditation or no meditation, he and John had busily set about tackling that very problem. "Paul couldn't let it rest, not even in India," Bob Spitz wrote. "Paul wrote like mad in Rishikesh—but truth be told, so did John."

Old habits die hard. Between them, working in secret—work was not allowed at the ashram—the two created almost 40 songs, compositions such as "Julia," "Mean Mr. Mustard," "Across the Universe" and "I'm So Tired" (John), and "Rocky Raccoon," "Mother Nature's Son," "Back in the U.S.S.R." and "Ob-La-Di, Ob-La-Da" (Paul). In all, they created enough music for two or three new albums, but when Paul broached the subject of their next LP with George, Harrison snarled at him. "I remember talking about the next album," Paul recalled, "and he would say: 'We're not here to talk music—we're here to meditate.' Oh, yeah, all right, Georgie Boy. Calm down, man."

Light and floating feelings were all well and good, but it was time to get back to business.

APPLE, THE COMPANY THE BEATLES formed long before Apple computers came on the scene, was conceived in a haze of '60s expansiveness. The corporation, meant to be as un-corporate as possible, was to be many things: an electronics firm, a clothing designer and store, a movie studio, a record label. It was in the latter role—and mainly, at first, as a developer of new musical talent—that the company was most successful. Paul, as always, was the driving force.

Peter Asher, whom Paul had brought in to help run the new label, remembered "hanging out a lot at Cavendish Avenue in the evenings, when [Paul] would be talking about Apple and his plans. He had some big colored diagrams he'd done of how Apple would work and be structured and all the things it could accomplish. He asked me first if I would produce some records for Apple, and then if I would be head of A&R for the label, and I happily accepted."

Paul played bass on the debut album of Asher's first major musical discovery, James Taylor. McCartney also signed the band Badfinger (whom he gave a song he'd tossed off, "Come and Get It") and the singer Mary Hopkin, who had a mammoth hit with "Those Were the Days." The company, it seemed, was off and running.

John and Paul went to New York in May to promote Apple; at a hotel press conference, Lin-

In 1968, the band visits the Maharishi in India for a three-month program of spiritual education, joined by the Beach Boys' Mike Love, Mia Farrow and Donovan. They are supposed to be meditating, but secretly, Paul and John are busy writing songs like "Across the Universe" and "Rocky Racoon." George, the most devout among them, is annoyed.

**By the time they record *The White Album*, in 1968, the mates
are still playing music together, but the boys' club is breaking up.
The songs have become individual efforts.**

da Eastman showed up and slipped Paul her phone number. "He rang me up later that day and told me they were leaving that evening, but he'd like it if I was able to travel out to the airport with him and John," she wrote years later, recalling the step they'd taken toward the inevitable.

Meanwhile, Yoko Ono was homing in on Lennon, "drawn both to John and to the girth of his bankbook, which could endow her [artistic] career," Bob Spitz wrote. Cynthia Lennon had wanted to accompany John to New York, but her increasingly remote husband said no. Instead, she went to Greece for vacation. When John returned to London and found the house empty, he invited Yoko over. Cynthia returned, according to Howard Sounes, "to find her husband and his Japanese lover sitting in bathrobes in her sunroom, having been up all night making music and making love."

Paul and John were both headed for seismic changes in their lives, in more ways than two.

THE WHITE ALBUM, the group's ninth (it was officially known simply as *The Beatles*), was filled with brilliancies, yet it couldn't have been a less group-like enterprise. The boys' club was breaking up: the boys were now thinking as individual men. "The songs were bolder and more emotional, though less self-conscious than *Revolver* and *Sgt. Pepper's*," according to Spitz. "And yet, there was clearly something uneven in their collective tone, something that seemed to pit the songs against one another ... The new repertoire, almost to a song, had lost its collaborative aspect. They were individual efforts—John's songs, Paul's songs, George's songs, written alone—and bore few of the familiar qualities that identified them as Beatles songs."

The group recorded the double LP's 30 songs together, even as outer and inner forces were starting to shake them apart. For one thing, John was in the grips of an incipient heroin addiction; for another, he was falling in love with Yoko Ono, whom he insisted on bringing into the recording studio. She sat glued by his side at all times, sometimes even contributing musical suggestions in blatant defiance of an unwritten rule that excluded all outsiders.

Suddenly there was no more inside. John's double remoteness pushed away the other members of the group, especially Paul. George, who contributed just four songs (although one was the monumental "While My Guitar Gently Weeps"), felt increasingly superfluous. And where the increasingly at-odds John and Paul were concerned, Ringo felt like a kid helplessly watching his soon-to-divorce parents fight.

And fight they did. An EMI employee vividly remembered one altercation: "I could hear them going at it in the hall, and it was terrifying. Paul was positively livid, accusing John of being reckless, childish, sabotaging the group." John was unmoved.

And yet when he recorded what he later called "a throwaway song," "Glass Onion," he tossed in a strange line: "Here's another clue for you all/ The walrus was Paul." At a time when all the world was overinterpreting every syllable of every Beatles number, even listening to the records backward for secret messages, the reference to Lennon's oblique "I Am the Walrus" was unmistakable. And, according to John, completely deceptive. "I was having a laugh because there'd been so much gobbledy-gook about *Pepper*—play it backwards, and you stand on your head and all that," he said. "At that time, I was still in my love cloud with Yoko. I thought, 'Well, I'll just say something nice to Paul, that it's all right and you did a good job over these few years, holding us together.'"

The joke would have unintended consequences.

IN JUNE, PAUL attended his brother Mike's wedding in Liverpool with Jane. To all present, they seemed like a happy couple. Then she went back to a theater engagement in Bristol, and Paul traveled to Los Angeles to attend a Capitol Records sales conference (where he would inform the startled attendees that all future Beatles albums were going to be released on Apple Records). On a layover in New York, he left a message with Linda Eastman's answering service, saying that he was on his way to the Coast and could be contacted at the Beverly Hills Hotel.

Linda showed up at his hotel the next afternoon, unannounced, and moved in.

This was a surprise to Peggy Lipton, whom Paul had phoned when he arrived in L.A., begging her to come see

John's falling in love with Yoko Ono along with an incipient heroin addiction lead to a double remoteness from the band and altercations in the studio.

him. When she showed up, Beatles roadie Tony Bramwell asked her to wait outside Paul's room. After a while, he emerged—soon followed by Linda, who seemed amused rather than upset by Lipton's presence. This was a very different woman from Jane. Long-legged, voluptuous, and wise in the ways of the rock-'n'-roll world, Linda was a kind of elegant outlaw: an earth mother with a pedigree. It was a package that was extraordinarily attractive to McCartney—especially the mother part. "Paul was drawn to her in a completely relaxed way," Bramwell recalled. "It was a mood I'd never seen him in before."

One thing Paul and Linda had in common—which Paul and Jane definitely did not—was marijuana. Linda had brought a bag of grass with her, which the two smoked, growing closer and closer until, when Paul checked out the next day, he and Linda were, Bramwell said, "like Siamese twins, holding hands and gazing into each other's eyes all the way to the airport."

Paul marries Linda in 1969, accompanied by her daughter Heather. Were his 1968 lyrics to "Hey Jude," far right, a foreshadowing?

MICHAEL LINDSAY-HOGG first met the Beatles in 1966, just before the group's final tour, when they hired him to make short films of them performing two of their songs, "Paperback Writer" and "Rain"—in effect, the first music videos, long before MTV. As the director wrote in his memoir, he found "that their bond, at that time, was still closer than any stranger could intrude on." When Lindsay-Hogg came back to film a new Beatles song in September 1968, he found four very different men.

"Things had changed a lot between them," he recalled recently. "It was partly, I think, because they'd stopped touring, which is often what holds bands together. They'd started to live very separate lives. They certainly weren't working collaboratively in the way they had originally—they all were more or less writing songs of their own, which they then would bring in, and the others would perform almost to instruction: 'Here are the chords.'"

The song in this instance was "Hey Jude," which Paul said had been inspired by sympathy for little Julian Lennon, whose daddy had left him and his mother to move in with Yoko Ono. Yet while the mega-hit single was one of the greatest rock anthems ever written (and at seven-plus minutes, the longest), it was also one of the strangest. Sympathy may have been Paul's initial impulse, but lines like "You were made to go out and get her" had nothing to do with a bereft boy. The always self-involved John took the song as a direct reference to him: "If you think about it," he said, "Yoko's just come into the picture. He's saying, 'Hey, Jude—Hey, John.'"

Not only does Linda have an extraordinary effect on Paul, but her camera also documents it, as in the photo above. Linda is a kind of elegant outlaw: an earth mother with a pedigree. Recalls a Beatles roadie: "Paul was drawn to her in a completely relaxed way."

But—if a single meaning can be given to the song—Linda Eastman had also just come into the picture, and Jane Asher was on her way out. It was an exciting, frightening and remorseful time in the composer's life. Was Paul—whose songs could be every bit as autobiographical as John's, if in a more veiled way—talking about himself when he counseled "Jude" not to be afraid but just to go and get her?

And then there was this very odd line: "You're waiting for someone to perform with."

Paul had found her. That Christmas, he asked Linda to marry him, and she accepted.

PERFORMING WAS THE germ of Paul's concept for the album *Let It Be* (which, though it was recorded before *Abbey Road,* would be released afterward, becoming the Beatles' swan song). Paul's idea was for the group to give its first concert since Candlestick Park, a show consisting of entirely new material, and to have Michael Lindsay-Hogg film both

The most famous bandmates in the world, in 1969, living out separate lives and barely tolerating one another, pose not long before the final breakup.

rehearsals and concert. It was an exciting, brand-new notion; it was also a desperate attempt on McCartney's part to glue the exploding band back together. The concert idea slowly fell apart because none of the four could agree on where, or even whether, to do it—or on much of anything else, for that matter. But the movie continued: maybe, Paul thought, it could be a documentary of the band recording its new material.

At the beginning of 1969, Lindsay-Hogg started filming on a soundstage outside London; he shot hundreds of hours of rehearsals, recording sessions and arguments. The Beatles eventually blocked the release of much of the footage, but some bits that have survived are as painful to watch as they must have been to live through. At one point, during a rehearsal of McCartney's song "Two of Us," Paul instructs a clearly irritated George on how his guitar accompaniment should sound. "I'll play whatever you want me to play, or I won't play at all if you don't want me to play," Harrison says. "Whatever it is that will please you, I'll do it."

Then he walked out.

After a few days, the other three persuaded George to come back. He returned on the condition that recording and filming be moved from the movie studio, which he hated, to the basement of Apple headquarters in London. He also brought along the keyboardist Billy Preston, an old friend of the band's from the Hamburg days, to sit in with the Beatles.

"[T]he presence of a guest had a civilizing influence on the band, as did a visit from Linda and Heather," Howard Sounes wrote. Linda's 6-year-old daughter bashed on Ringo's drums, laughed when Ringo held his ears and danced while the group happily rocked through a couple of covers from the old days, "Besame Mucho" and Little Richard's "Lawdy Miss Clawdy." "Heather danced around and around until she fell over giddy, the Beatles smiling at each other over their instruments." The touchstone memory of the band's beginnings, when the four young men from Liverpool had nothing but the music and each other, had restored order.

Until Lindsay-Hogg proposed a concert ending to the film. To be shot on the roof of the Apple building. The lunchtime crowds below would be the audience—just like at the Cavern in the old days, only farther away.

There was tentative agreement at first, and then there wasn't. "On Thursday, Jan. 30, 1969," Lindsay-Hogg wrote, "the Beatles, Yoko, and I gathered about noon in a small room off the wooden staircase leading to the roof, and to my dismay, I realized the enterprise was not secure."

George didn't see the point. Ringo remarked on how cold it was up there.

"'Come on, lads,' Paul said. 'It'll be fun,' enthusiasm covering the hard muscle of his determination. 'Let's do *something*.'"

But no one moved, Lindsay-Hogg recalled; time froze until all eyes turned to John. "Let's do it," he said.

"And so," the director wrote, "the Beatles climbed the narrow staircase to the roof and into history.

"The concert on the roof was the last time the Beatles ever played together to any kind of audience. It was their final performance, their good-bye, although none of us knew it.

"And the wonderful thing was that they were happy, dispute and rancor forgotten. In the 40 minutes we were up there, on that cold winter's day, they rocked and rolled and connected as they had in years gone by, friends again. It was beautiful to see.

"When it was over, John stepped to the mike and said, 'I'd like to say thank you on behalf of the group and ourselves, and I hope we passed the audition.'"

On a cold January day in 1969, the Beatles come together on the roof of Apple Corps headquarters in London for their last public performance as a group.

When I'm Sixty-Four

IN THE NOV. 7, 1969, ISSUE OF *LIFE*, PAUL McCartney responded to a piece of urban mythology that had spread around the world like wildfire that fall, stoked by various "clues" on Beatles albums (including John's "walrus" lyric): Paul had died in a 1966 car wreck and been replaced by a look-alike. (The look-alike would also have been one amazing sound-alike.) "Perhaps the rumor started because I haven't been much in the press lately," Paul said. "I have done enough press for a lifetime, and I

don't have anything to say these days. I am happy to be with my family, and I will work when I work. I was switched on for 10 years, and I never switched off. Now I am switching off whenever I can. I would rather be a little less famous these days."

The magazine's cover was a cozily domestic black-and-white photo of Paul and his new family at High Park, the Scottish farm he'd bought in 1966: one arm nestling Linda—the two had married in March, eight days before John Lennon married Yoko Ono—and the other cradling

Paul and his daughter Mary in the family garden around the time of his first solo album, *McCartney*. Mary has become a photographer, like her mother.

In 1969, near EMI studios on Abbey Road, the four prepare to cross into history with the photo that became an icon. At this point, Paul, barefoot on the album cover, still has his sandals on.

their 2-month-old daughter Mary (named after Paul's mother). In front of them stands Linda's young daughter Heather, whom McCartney would later adopt. Paul looks scruffy and slightly puffy, happy if a little dazed. Linda, with her golden tresses and high cheekbones, looks smashing. Heather wields a shepherd's crook, as if to ward off intruders.

Paul's dazed expression was well earned. He'd been through a hell of a year, and the death rumor was the least of it. The disintegration of the band that had meant everything to him, and to the world, was inching toward its inevitable climax—even as the Beatles started to record *Abbey Road,* the last album they would make together. Symbolizing the breakdown was the group's inability to agree on a financial adviser, a position they badly needed to fill to sort out the giant mess Apple had become. John Lennon, who had come out of his heroin and LSD haze and was now bridling at Paul's leadership of the Beatles, wanted to hire the Rolling Stones' co-manager, a brilliant but abrasive New Jersey accountant named Allen Klein. Paul wanted his new father-in-law, high-powered New York entertainment lawyer Lee Eastman, for the job. Paul's choice seemed like a conflict of interest to the other Beatles, who feared Eastman would favor McCartney. Lennon convinced George and Ringo that Klein, whose blue-collar style all three trusted, was their man. Klein was hired, over Paul's protests. Meanwhile, Paul retained Eastman as Apple's corporate counsel. Epic clashes followed.

"You just don't know how horrible it was at Apple in that period," recalled Apple Corps press officer Tony Bramwell. "It was like being in the middle of a gigantic divorce ... On one phone, you'd have John asking you to do this; on the other phone, you'd have Paul asking you to do [something else]. By then George and Ringo had washed their hands of it."

Small wonder, then, that Paul hadn't invited any of the other Beatles to his wedding. "Why not? I'm a total bastard, I suppose," he said. "I don't know, really. Maybe it was because the group was breaking up. We were all pissed off with each other. We certainly weren't a gang any more. That was the thing. Once a group's broken up like that, that's it."

In the midst of it all, to blow off steam, Paul recorded a song called "My Dark Hour" with rocker Steve Miller. "My dark hour, Mother Nature's child/ My dark hour, oh, it's drivin' me wild" went one line. McCartney, an excellent drummer, did the percussion on the track and, as Miller recalled, "really beat the hell out of those drums."

And in the midst of it all and in spite of everything, *Abbey Road* came together. George Martin had wanted to make the album a continuous tapestry of sound; Lennon, the inveterate rock 'n' roller, wanted it to consist of discrete three-minute tracks—with, as appropriate to the divorce in progress, his songs on one side and Paul's on the other. A compromise was reached:

individual songs by John, Paul, George and Ringo on one side of the LP; a long medley of inter-woven fragments on the other.

It worked. "We were holding it together," Paul said. "The music was O.K., and we were friends enough that, even though this undercurrent was going on, we still had a strong respect for each other even at the very worst points." And there were best points: with the great "Some-thing" and "Here Comes the Sun," Harrison was finally coming into his own as a songwriter on a par with Lennon and McCartney, even as the group was ending. John's "Come Together," bol-stered by Paul's magnificently muddy, menacing bass line, was one of Lennon's greatest songs. And the side-2 medley, knitted together by McCartney and Martin, was a towering achieve-ment, one that has influenced popular music for the past 40 years. "George Martin, being the brilliant producer that he is, figured out how to sew this all together and make it be one thing," Billy Joel said recently. "It was patchwork. It was a quilt. I heard this, and I went, 'Wow! What a great idea.'"

While working on *Abbey Road*, the writing duo's last album together, "we still had a strong respect for each other, even at the very worst points," said Paul.

The album's final song was fittingly climactic. "In 'The End,' there were three guitar solos where John, George and I took a line each, which was something we'd never done before," Paul said. "And we finally persuaded Ringo to lay a drum solo, which he'd never wanted to do." Then came *Abbey Road*'s final state-ment, written and sung by Paul: "And in the end, the love you take is equal to the love you make."

Even John had to admit: "A very cosmic, philo-sophical line."

And then it really was the end. In September, Len-non told the others, "I want a divorce." "For about three or four months, George, Ringo and I rang each other to ask: 'Well, is this it then?'" Paul recalled. "Nobody quite knew if it was just one of John's little flings, and that maybe he was going to feel the pinch in a week's time and say, 'I was only kidding ...' So we held on to that thread for a few months, and then eventually we real-ized, 'Oh, well, we're not in the band anymore. That's it. It's definitely over.'"

Paul took the loss hardest of all. "It was a pretty good job to have lost—the Beatles," he said. "My whole life since I'd been 17 had been wrapped up in it, so it was quite a shock. I took to my bed, didn't bother shaving much, did a lot of drinking … So I lost the plot there for a little while—for about a year, actually—but luckily Linda's very sensible, and she said, 'Look, you're O.K.' I was thinking, 'Well, can I ever write and sing again? What does anyone want with an out-of-work bass player?' It hit me pretty hard."

It was harder than that. "I nearly had a breakdown," he told his daughter Mary, years later in a documentary. "I was going crazy."

Linda pulled him out of it. Though there must have been times, living with an infant, a 7-year-old and a severely depressed husband on a remote Scottish farm, when she wondered what she'd taken on, she was tough and practical. She "told Paul there was a way forward,"

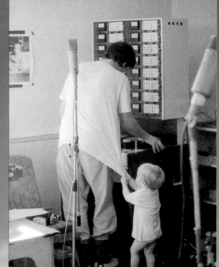

With the Beatles no longer his nuclear family, Paul sets about building a domestic life. On his farm in Scotland, far left, he bundles his daughter Mary for a photo, taken by Linda, that appears on the cover of his first solo album; below, Paul gambols in the countryside with Linda, who helped pull him out of his post-Beatles depression; work in the studio becomes a family affair, with son James tagging along in 1979.

PHOTOGRAPH BY HARRY BENSON

Howard Sounes writes. "He could make music without the Beatles. She would help, if he liked."

Paul listened. "After a while, I thought, 'Jesus! I had better really try to get it together here,' and that took the form of making a record, the simplest way … a real homegrown record; working on my own, thinking of getting a new band—although, obviously, the Beatles was a tough act to follow."

THE RECORD WAS *McCARTNEY*, his first solo album, and it really was homegrown: Paul recorded it at Cavendish Avenue and, as secretly as possible, at Abbey Road and another studio on the outskirts of London. "We decided we didn't want to tell anyone what we were doing," he later told *Rolling Stone*. "That way it gets to be like home at the studio." Barry Miles writes, "Linda would make the booking, and they would arrive with sandwiches and a bottle of grape juice, put the baby on the floor, give Heather her toys and start to make music. It felt like a holiday compared to the atmosphere that had attended Beatles recording sessions for the previous two years."

But the Beatles still hung around his neck like a millstone. Though the members of the band knew it was over, the outside world hadn't been officially told yet—and then there was the letter of the law. Upon the formation of Apple, in 1967, the four had signed a contract binding them together financially for 10 years. And Allen Klein, who was now in control of Apple, directed that *McCartney*—which was on the Apple label—was not to be released before *Let It Be,* which was still in process.

Paul was furious. When Ringo came to his house to deliver the news on behalf of the others, "I did something I never did before or since: I told him to get out," Paul said. In the end, the release date of *Let It Be* was pushed up, and *McCartney* came out as originally scheduled, on April 17, 1970.

The album certainly was homespun—its first track, "The Lovely Linda," was an ad lib Paul had used to test the recording equipment—and the critics were tough. "With this record, his debt to George Martin becomes increasingly clear," *Melody Maker's* critic said, citing the "sheer banality" of the tunes (many of them instrumentals), except one: "Maybe I'm Amazed," a gorgeous love song to Linda and an instant classic. Whatever McCartney's debt to Martin—or to John Lennon, for that matter—his genius as a writer of melody ranked with that of any composer, pop or classical.

McCartney rose to the top of the charts in the U.S., but it made an even bigger splash before its release. Paul, unable to bear interviews since the ugliness with his former bandmates had begun, included a Q&A with Apple board member Peter Brown with press copies of the album. The end of the questionnaire created a sensation.

PETER BROWN: Is your break with the Beatles temporary or permanent, due to personal differences or musical ones?

PAUL: Personal differences, business differences, but most of all because I have a better time with my family. Temporary or permanent? I don't know.

PETER BROWN: Do you foresee a time when Lennon-McCartney becomes an active songwriting partnership again?

PAUL: No.

The breakup had been private until that moment. Paul had let the cat out of the bag. "So

Paul, here with his dog Lucky in 1971, pursues a bucolic life at farms in
Scotland and Sussex, near London, surrounding himself with animals,
including cows, chickens, horses and sheep.

I was not loved for that by the other guys," he said, "and that started a war between us." John,
George and Ringo accused Paul of using the announcement to publicize his new album. Paul
accused John of cowardice for not having gone public when Lennon left the group six months
earlier. The sniping would go back and forth for years. Soon McCartney would sue Allen Klein—
and his former bandmates—to divorce himself commercially from the group. Eventually, John,
George and Ringo fell out with Klein as well. In the end, the four men who'd been closer to one
another than to anyone else in the world would also mend fences. But it would take time.

And gradually the world grew out of its initial shock and outrage at the Beatles' dissolution.
It was the end of a glorious dream, and the temptation to find a scapegoat was overpowering.
Yoko Ono was the initial candidate. But let Ringo, the Sensible One, have the last word on the
matter. "Yoko's taken a lot of shit, her and Linda," he said, "but the Beatles' breakup wasn't their
fault. It was just that suddenly we were all 30 and married and changed. We couldn't carry on
that life anymore."

PAUL'S INITIAL REACTION when Life's reporter and photographer
showed up at High Park had been outrage and fury at the invasion of his privacy: he'd thrown
a bucket of water at the pair and taken a swing at the photographer, who caught the moment
on film. Coming to his senses, McCartney struck a bargain with the team. If they gave him
the offending roll of film, he and his family would pose for a picture (no wonder Heather was
swinging that shepherd's crook), and he would sit for a brief interview.

After dismissing the "Paul Is Dead" rumor, he said, "The Beatle thing is over. It has been exploded, partly by what we have done and partly by other people. We are individuals, all different. John married Yoko; I married Linda. We didn't marry the same girl ... Can you spread it around that I am just an ordinary person, and I want to live in peace?"

The paradox of Paul McCartney was—and always has been—that he is both an ordinary and an extraordinary person in one man's body. But with Linda's help, he slowly began to find some peace. His center of gravity in the years just after the Beatles breakup was his Scottish farm: a couple of hundred acres of rolling meadow in hilly, rocky country on the remote Kintyre peninsula. The farm's only buildings were a rustic, one-story stone house (without heat or hot water) and a barn; there were some cows, chickens and horses, and a small herd of black-faced sheep. Paul made friends with the neighboring farmers and hired a caretaker to watch his place when he wasn't there. The locals grew protective of his privacy and were vague about his location when reporters or stray Beatles fans came nosing around.

Always a perfectionist, Paul wanted to move on from *McCartney,* whose almost tossed-off quality reflected a man coming out of a post-traumatic daze. In the fall of 1970, he took his family to New York—they stayed at Linda's old apartment—and very purposefully set about making a new album.

Ram was a very different album from *McCartney,* filled with emotions, not all of them sunny. "I really think that *Ram* was all the angst coming out," said Denny Seiwell, the new drummer

Critics are cruel about the Ram album, one calling it "inconsequential," but it sells well. The world misses the Beatles.

Paul had hired. McCartney being McCartney, however, the angst was transmuted into highly tuneful form. Listen carefully to the delightful "Too Many People," and you'll hear two lines Paul later admitted were directed squarely at John: "Too many people preaching practices" and, more pointedly, "You took your lucky break/ And broke it in two." But the main story *Ram* told was one of Paul and Linda's intense new couplehood. Not only were half the album's songs credited to Paul and Linda McCartney (some said this was Paul's way of evading a contract clause that bound all his solo compositions to Apple until 1973), but Linda was also on the record in a far more pronounced way. On *McCartney,* she'd tentatively sung along on a couple of tracks; on *Ram,* she was virtually her husband's co-vocalist, especially on "Ram On" and the *Sgt. Pepper*-y pastiche "Uncle Albert/ Admiral Halsey" (which whimsically referred to an actual uncle of Paul's).

Could she really sing? As long as you didn't listen too hard, some of the harmonies—while far from Lennon/McCartney/Harrison at their gorgeous prime—were actually kind of sweet. And if Linda's pitch wavered a little here and there ("She wasn't spot on a lot of the time," Seiwell said. "But we would just work with what we could, and she did improve over the years"), well, that was kind of sweet, too, if you had a romantic bone in your body. They were doing it for love.

Still, love wasn't the same thing as art, and while *Ram* sold very well, reaching No. 1 in the U.K. and No. 2 in the U.S., the critics were cruel. *Rolling Stone* called the album "incredibly inconsequential" and "monumentally irrelevant." Such refusals to take McCartney on his own terms reflected the pain of the world at large at the fact that the Beatles weren't going to be making any more records.

But the world was in no greater pain than the three other former Beatles, who were now embroiled in legal battles with the man who had been their drill sergeant, schoolteacher and presiding co-genius. All of them, even the friendly Ringo, took potshots at *Ram*: "I feel sad about Paul's albums," Starr told *Melody Maker*. "I don't think there's one [good] tune on the last one, *Ram* ... he seems to be going strange."

Though no stranger than John Lennon, who was also in love and also bringing out his debut solo album, *John Lennon/Plastic Ono Band*. John and Yoko had recently undergone so-called primal therapy, which involved screaming out childhood traumas during consultations, and John had carried his cries of anguish into such new songs as "Mother" and "Working Class Hero." But anguish turned to rage and contempt when John heard *Ram,* which he perceived as being full of attacks on him, as well as the kind of McCartney fluff he'd always detested.

The result was "How Do You Sleep?"—a direct broadside at Paul, which appeared on John's next album, *Imagine,* and contained the lines, "Those freaks was right when they said you was dead" and "The only thing you done was yesterday/ And since you've gone you're just another day." Years later, Lennon claimed to have been writing about himself as much as about McCartney in the song, and said, "I wasn't really feeling that vicious at the time." But he went on to say, "I think Paul died creatively, in a way."

This is harsh, and while it contains elements of truth, it's also the cry of a spurned lover—a role both John and Paul would continue to play, with various degrees of overtness, until John's death. Unlike Rodgers and Hammerstein, the great songwriting team whose creativity and commercial success Lennon and McCartney had half-jokingly aspired to, the former best friends from Liverpool were both composer-lyricists, each with a strong point and an Achilles heel: respectively, lyrics and melody for John, and the reverse for Paul. Interviewed shortly before his death, Lennon made an intriguing statement about his old partner: "Paul is quite a capable lyricist who doesn't think he is," John said. "So he doesn't go for it. Rather than face the problem, he would avoid it."

Paul was a great one for tackling practical problems head-on—the Beatles' financial problems, say—and less great at handling emotional issues: his mother's death, his breakup with Jane (and with John). Competitiveness with Lennon had often forced his hand in songwriting and coaxed out some of his strongest lyrics: "Yesterday," "Eleanor Rigby," "Penny Lane." Now that the competition was officially over, now that they were no longer playing into each other's noses, as John had memorably put it, Paul had shifted into another lyrical key.

"Another Day," his first post-Beatles single, set a pattern. The lyric was literary, in that it was based on a character (a device that Lennon, who wrote about himself, avoided at all costs): a lonely working woman—"'Eleanor Rigby' in New York City," Denny Seiwell said. But "Another Day" was "Eleanor Rigby" lite, dealing with garden-variety melancholy instead of life and death. "So sad, so sad/ Sometimes she feels so sad" could describe anybody. The words blew away rather than biting in.

The melody was another matter. "Another Day" was just insanely catchy. No one could write a hook like Paul McCartney. The song's chart performance—No. 2 in the U.K., No. 4 in the U.S.—showed that even if he was no longer getting people where they lived, he was still getting them.

AND NOW HE WANTED ANOTHER BAND. In the waning days of the Beatles, Paul had dreamed of taking the group back to its roots: the happy, scruffy, pre-mania days when the four of them had traveled up and down England in their jeans and leather jackets, simply making rock 'n' roll and taking life as it came. Couldn't the four of them

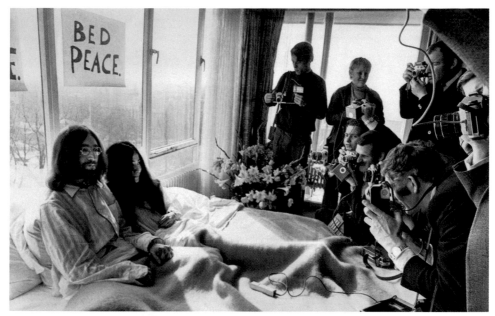

As the Beatles spin apart in 1969, John and Yoko become a performing duo of their own, notably staging their Bed-Ins for Peace, the first one taking place during their honeymoon in Amsterdam.

just tour again, playing small venues and moving on fast to the next destination? It was a sweet thought, but it was sheer nostalgia—between fame and discord, out of the question.

Now, though, maybe something like it was possible. A small touring band ... drummer Seiwell was already onboard, as was backup vocalist Linda Eastman McCartney, whom Paul had tried to forge into a keyboardist as well, without much success. Clearly, another musician was needed, one who was as close as possible to Paul's abilities but wouldn't vie for leadership. Paul chose Denny Laine, a talented vocalist and multi-instrumentalist who'd co-founded, then quit, the Moody Blues a few years earlier.

Soon after Laine came on board, Linda gave birth, by emergency cesarean, to the couple's second child, Stella. It was a difficult birth, imperiling both mother and child, and when both came through safely, Paul said he'd imagined a guardian angel protecting the family. The image gave him an idea for the name of his new band.

Wings threw together a first album, *Wild Life,* working fast and loose—five of the record's tracks were first takes. The record had a loose, garage-y feel: the essence of its appeal to those who liked it; the root of its failure to those who didn't. Whatever the critics said, though, McCartney seemed not to be phoning it in but trying hard for a credible post-Beatles sound.

Gradually, Paul's dream materialized. After a new guitarist named Henry McCullough joined the band, Wings piled into a rented van in London and headed north on a kind of neo-Magical Mystery Tour, showing up unannounced at college campuses and booking itself on the spot. At its first stop, the University of Nottingham, Wings played Elvis and Little Richard covers—no Beatles songs—and charged 40 new pence (61¢) a ticket. That summer, the band toured Europe in a brightly colored, double-decker bus with the McCartney kids onboard and a big sign on the side that read WINGS OVER EUROPE. They were still playing small venues, building up road experience before going on to anything more ambitious and generally having a blast.

Until they got to Sweden. As Paul and Linda toured, they'd had their regular marijuana supply sent through Denny Seiwell by mail rather than risk passing the drug through customs; in Gothenburg in August, the three of them were caught and fined £1,000. The following month, Scottish police found cannabis growing on the McCartneys' farm; Paul and Linda were fined once more. The busts made headlines, resulted in the cancellation of a planned Wings tour and were a harbinger of annoyances to come.

THE YEAR 1973 marked several key passages in McCartney's life. That spring, the Cavern was demolished during the construction of a ventilation shaft for a subway that was never built. The needless destruction seemed all too symbolic: of a city that was struggling financially; of the way Liverpool seemed to have written off—for the time being, at least—the four local boys who'd made it big and moved away.

Paul, though, maintained his ties to Merseyside, returning often to visit his father (who'd remarried) and his large extended family, many of whom he helped—and still helps—financially.

That year, Paul also bought another rural retreat, with a circular house called Waterfall, deep in the Sussex countryside, 60 miles south of London. Soon he would buy the adjacent property, Blossom Wood Farm, where he built a larger house: he and his growing family would spend more and more time there over the years.

He also made another important purchase, on the suggestion of Lee Eastman: the song catalog of one of his early idols, Buddy Holly. Paul would continue to scoop up the catalogs of various songwriters, greatly increasing his fortune and compensating, in a way, for his inability to secure the rights to the Lennon-McCartney catalog, which had slipped away amid his legal tussles with his former bandmates and would remain tantalizingly out of reach. (It would eventually be bought by Michael Jackson.)

That summer saw the release of two new Wings singles, the syrupy "My Love" and the galvanizing "Live and Let Die," the latter reuniting Paul with George Martin, to grand effect. Both songs were international hits, and "Live and Let Die," the theme song of the James Bond movie of the same name, would be nominated for an Academy Award. It remains in McCartney's concert repertoire to this day.

And that summer, Wings recorded its best album to date, *Band on the Run*—minus Denny Seiwell and Henry McCullough, who quit at the last minute over artistic and financial differences. The musicians' felt that Paul needed to control every note that was played in the studio, and they were discontent about money (he paid the players a nominal salary and middling bonuses). Although *Band on the Run* was essentially made (with later overdubs) by a two-man band, McCartney and Laine, it garnered the first uniformly positive reviews for a Wings album and began to change the critics' estimation of Paul as an over-the-hill hack.

WINGS FLEW ON THROUGH THE '70S, through tours, albums, singles and personnel changes. There were high points (14 Top 10 singles, including six No. 1's, in the U.S.; "Jet," "Listen to What the Man Said," "Mull of Kintyre") and low points (Paul and Linda's mullets; "Silly Love Songs," "Mull of Kintyre"). The decade was a remarkably active one for McCartney, as he continued to explore musically and push relentlessly for commercial success. His drive, given the considerable laurels he could have rested on, was beyond remarkable: it was almost vengeful. It was as if he were showing something to all the people who'd accused him of trying to rule the Beatles, of being melodically saccharine and lyrically mediocre.

By 1973, Wings is in full flight, with Linda in the band, touring extensively and pumping out hits. In the summer, Wings releases *Band on the Run*, garnering its first uniformly positive album reviews.

The problem was that like most over-compensators, he had many of those same feelings about himself, especially where Wings was concerned. "I used to think that all my Wings stuff was second-rate," he told *Playboy* in the mid-'80s. "[But] no matter what I may think about them … I can view them cynically, even ruthlessly … even I have to admit there definitely was something there with some of the Wings songs. In fact, the more I bother looking at it again, the more I discover what I was trying to do."

Even Paul's most ardent fans, though, wondered what he was trying to do when he put his nonmusician wife square in the middle of the band—and in the critical crosshairs. "Well, we laid ourselves open to that kind of criticism," he admitted. "But it was out of complete innocence that I got Wings together and naively said, 'Come on, Lin, do you want to be in it?' But looking back on it, I can understand the criticism," McCartney said. "If we were doing it again, we just might be more thoughtful. But I'm proud of her. I really threw her in the deep end."

Linda's own feelings about her tenure in the band were mixed at best. "I don't quite know how I had the nerve to join [Paul]," she told *Playboy*. "I mean, how do you go out with Beethoven and say, 'Sure, I'll sing harmony with you,' when you've never sung a note? Or 'Sure, I'll play piano with you,' when you've never played? It was mad. But I'm … enthusiastic about things. Isn't it funny? People write that I'm cold and pushy. I hope I'm not, but I have that kind of face … I don't smile a lot. The truth is, I'm an old softy."

There were those who found her arrogant, tough and demanding—but in these things, she was well matched with her husband. Like Paul, she could be thoroughly charming when the occasion, or the company, demanded.

"Linda was a girl from New York," says Michael Lindsay-Hogg, who after directing *Let It Be,* made videos of several McCartney songs (including "Mull of Kintyre") and was friendly with Paul and his family. "A lot of people found her slightly abrasive and tactless. I'm not sure that tact was her strong suit. But 'tact' is just another word for not being direct. I liked her very much. I made her laugh, and she made me laugh. I got Linda, and I thought she was good for Paul.

"He seemed to want a stable relationship," Lindsay-Hogg says. "He seemed to go for a wife and children, as opposed to flitting around and being promiscuous. I think Paul always liked that traditional setup because it made it easy for him to keep on working, which is, of course, what he's done all his life."

IN THE FLUSH OF COMMERCIAL SUCCESS and domestic happiness, Paul began to try to patch things up with John Lennon. It wasn't easy—though nothing about Lennon was ever easy. He and Yoko Ono had moved to New York City and bought an apartment in the Dakota, an eccentric old building overlooking Central Park. But in 1973, they hit a rough patch in their marriage, and Lennon moved out, traveling to the West Coast with his and Yoko's assistant, a young woman named May Pang.

John, who was drinking and drugging heavily then, later called the period his "lost weekend." But Paul, who had traveled to Los Angeles for the Academy Awards, where "Live and Let Die" was up for Best Song, found him, and their meetings were cordial. One night, they jammed together at a studio where Lennon was producing a record for singer/songwriter Harry Nilsson (who was also present, along with Stevie Wonder); the next day, Paul stopped by the house

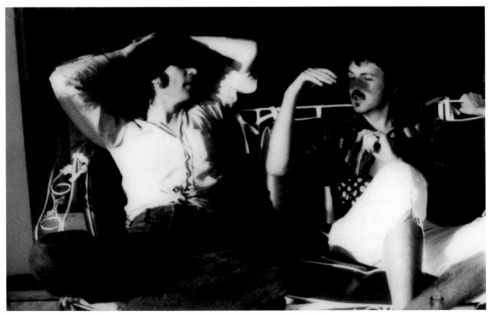

In one of the last photos of Lennon and McCartney together, Paul visits John in California, where he's gone with girlfriend May Pang after a breakup with Yoko. Paul confides to John that Yoko misses him.

where John was living with Pang and, according to Howard Sounes, "gave John some brotherly advice. He told him Yoko missed him, and if he felt the same, he should try to win her back."

John returned to New York and reconciled with Yoko, beginning what was to be a five-year retreat from public life (and recording); their son Sean was born the following October. That Christmas, Paul and Linda turned up on their doorstep at the Dakota, singing a carol. Within minutes, recalled rock-'n'-roll photographer Bob Gruen, who was visiting, John and Paul were "[h]ugging, patting each other on the back … like high school buddies who hadn't seen each other in a long time and really liked each other."

THREE MONTHS LATER, JIM McCARTNEY—who'd

washed clothes and dishes for his two motherless boys, who'd tickled the ivories and sung the old favorites at family gatherings, who'd looked slightly askance at his elder son and his daft friend while they strummed their guitars and crooned love songs in the little front room on Forthlin Road—died at home in Liverpool, at age 73. A lifelong smoker, he'd been in failing health. Paul, who was on his way to Copenhagen to begin a Wings European tour, didn't attend the funeral. "It's no coincidence that Paul was on the continent at the time," his brother Mike wrote. "Like Dad, who'd apologize for not being able to hold our stomachs when, as kids, we were being sick, Paul would never face that sort of thing. As Dad would say, 'It's just the way you're made, Son.'"

INCREASINGLY, PERHAPS not coincidentally, Paul began seeking out

John Lennon. Spending time in New York that spring, McCartney would frequently drop by the Dakota unannounced. One night he and John were watching *Saturday Night Live* when executive producer Lorne Michaels jocularly held up a check for $3,200, made out to the Beatles—the union rate for a band performance on *SNL*—and said it could all be theirs if they'd perform three songs on the show. "We went, 'Ha-ha, wouldn't it be funny if we went down?'" Lennon later recalled. "We nearly got into a cab, but we were actually too tired."

It was a time when hopeful talk of a Fab Four reunion was in the air, but too much water had flowed under the bridge; too many hurt feelings had been stirred up—ultimately, it was just talk. John had moved on. "That was a period when Paul just kept turning up at our door with a guitar," he recalled in 1980. "I would let him in, but finally I said to him, 'Please call before you come over. It's not 1956, and turning up at the door isn't the same anymore. You know, just give me a ring.' He was upset by that, but I didn't mean it badly. I just meant that I was taking care of a baby all day, and some guy turns up at the door."

"The sad thing," Linda said, four years after John's death, "is that John and Paul both had problems, and they loved each other, and, boy, could they have helped each other! … I know that Paul was desperate to write with John again. And I know John was desperate to write. Desperate. People thought, 'Well, he's taking care of Sean. He's a house-husband and all that.' But he wasn't happy. He couldn't write, and it drove him crazy. And Paul could have helped him … easily."

And by helping John, Paul could have helped himself. With his incomparable ear, he knew that the music he was making wasn't even close to the standard of Lennon-McCartney. The paradox was that he was a raging success, especially compared with the other ex-Beatles: "After a strong start with *All Things Must Pass,* Harrison's career had fallen flat," Sounes writes. "Lennon had enjoyed chart success, but he'd also released flop albums, and he didn't tour … And Ritchie was never going to be anything but a novelty act. Paul was leaving the boys in his dust.

He had always been the most hard-working Beatle, the most prolific and focused. He was also the one who really enjoyed live performance, and he had the happy knack of being able to write hits whenever he pleased."

NINETEEN-EIGHTY BEGAN BADLY. After Paul's people had gone to great lengths to secure visas for Wings for a lucrative tour of Japan—both McCartney and Denny Laine had been busted for pot in years past—customs officials found a plastic bag containing almost eight ounces of marijuana among the shirts in Paul's suitcase, and he was hustled off to jail in handcuffs.

This was no slap on the wrist. Drug possession was a grave offense in Japan, and Paul faced a prison sentence. The nine days that followed were among the most difficult in his life. At first, he slept with his back to the wall, fearing rape. Linda was trapped in their hotel with the four kids (the youngest, 2-year-old James, had been born in 1977), fearing the worst. The rest of the band was told to leave the country; the tour was history. The instruments were shipped home. The headlines blared.

Paul, being Paul, made the best of the situation. He meditated. At one point, during a group shower, he led the other inmates in a sing-along, crooning "Yellow Submarine" to great effect. Finally, his brother-in-law John Eastman and the British consul persuaded the Japanese government to let its famous prisoner go, on the condition that he make a full confession and not return to the country for seven years.

Paul never apologized to the members of his band, who lost considerable income as a result of the fiasco; the episode was the beginning of the end for Wings. In the meantime, he released a solo album, *McCartney II,* and set to work on another one, *Tug of War,* with George Martin.

And that fall, John Lennon brought out his first album in five years, *Double Fantasy,* in time for his 40th birthday. Though the album's concept—alternating tracks by John and Yoko—militated against commercial success, Lennon's raw and honest voice was once again on the radio airwaves. Songs like the world-weary "Watching the Wheels," about the costs of fame, and the blissful "Beautiful Boy (Darling Boy)," John's hymn to 5-year-old Sean, packed an emotional weight far more powerful than the seductive, upbeat charms of Paul's best-selling "Coming Up."

Then, on Dec. 8, John's voice was stilled forever.

EVEN FOUR YEARS ON, Paul could barely discuss his partner's death. "I feel that if I said anything about John, I would have to sit here for five days and say it all," he told *Playboy* in 1984. "Or I don't want to say anything."

What he did say was that "strangely enough, all of us ... the three Beatles, friends of John's ... all of us reacted in the same way. Separately. Everyone just went to work that day. All of us. Nobody could stay home with that news. We all had to go to work and be with people we knew ... So I went in and did a day's work in a kind of shock. And as I was coming out of the studio later, there was a reporter, and as we were driving away, he just stuck the microphone in the window and shouted, 'What do you think about John's death?' I had just finished a whole day in shock, and I said, 'It's a drag.' I meant drag in the heaviest sense of the word, you know: 'It's a—DRAG.' But, you know, when you

look at that in print, it says, 'Yes, it's a drag.'"

Paul recalled that when his mother, a registered nurse, had died, he'd said, "What are we going to do for money?" "I never have quite forgiven myself for that," he told the interviewer. "But that's all I could say then. It's like a lot of kids; when you tell them someone's died, they laugh."

"Because they can't cope with the emotion?" the interviewer asked.

"Yes," Paul said. "Exactly."

In 1983, Paul records two duets with Michael Jackson, "The Girl Is Mine" and "Say, Say, Say," produced by former Beatles guru George Martin.

IN DEATH, JOHN became a saint, a larger-than-life figure, like Elvis—"Martin Luther Lennon," Paul sometimes called him, when he felt the world was laying on the idolatry too thick. Liverpudlians have a famously acerbic sense of humor, John being one of its prime exponents; Paul, for all his sunny music, was no slouch in that department.

And yet Liverpool itself underwent a sea change after Lennon's death. The hometown that had reviled the Beatles as ingrates, fugitives and drug addicts start-ed to come around. A mass public memo-

Superstars unite in 1985 for Live Aid, which concludes with Bob Geldof hoisted onto the shoulders of Pete Townshend and McCartney.

rial took place in the city that December; gradually, local feelings softened toward the prodigals. Perhaps they, or their memory, might even prove of some benefit.

John's memory certainly benefited his former bandmates. In the wake of his death, Beatles albums—reissued, repackaged, remastered—started to sell through the roof and have never really stopped since. (Even *Double Fantasy* went to No. 1.) With John's death, the former Fab Four went straight from illustrious has-beens to historical figures, endlessly aglow.

Yet Paul, who had the most currency (in both senses of the word) of any of them, found himself losing traction in the '80s. In 1982, *Tug of War* hit No. 1 in the U.S. and the U.K.—but was McCartney's last album to achieve the distinction. After Lennon's death, Paul stopped touring for several years, worried he would be the "next" to be killed, and took on other proj-ects, with varying degrees of success. He began painting, at first as a hobbyist and then more seriously. He produced and starred in a disastrous movie musical, *Give My Regards to Broad Street.* He recorded two duets with Michael Jackson, "The Girl Is Mine" and "Say Say Say"—and then reacted with helpless fury when Jackson, whom he had considered to be a friend, bought (for $47.5 million, part of the profits from *Thriller*) ATV Music, a publishing company that contained most of the Beatles' catalog.

In 1985, Paul performed "Let It Be" at Bob Geldof's world-televised Live Aid benefit: it was the first time he'd played onstage in five years. It was also the first of many benefits he would play in the years to come. And the following year, he released *Press to Play,* an album he was proud of—only to see it sell fewer than 1 million copies worldwide: a big flop, in Paul McCartney terms.

It was time to press RESET.

PAUL WICKENS—Wix, for short— was part of the band that Paul, under new management, assembled in 1989 to make, and tour, a new album, *Flowers in the Dirt.* By now, McCartney was living primarily on the family farm near Peasmarsh, Sussex; he'd also built a recording studio nearby, called Hog Hill Mill. There was little need for him to go up to London anymore, and the country life Wix Wickens found him living was lovely, if isolated. The McCartneys were a tight unit, sealed in by their fame. "It was run like a family home," he recently told TIME. "It's not a huge mansion—it's a lovely farmhouse in lovely grounds. And Linda was into her horses big-time. So they would go riding. They would grow things—[they had] an organic farm. In that sense, it was idyllic. They could eat their own produce. And their kids were in [public] school there. So it was a family home, with kids running around like a family. The difference was there was a very famous element to the family … But when you went there, it was just a welcoming family, with Linda cooking, and Paul was there playing a trumpet as you arrived to welcome you in."

The cooking was strictly vegetarian: the family had been dedicated meat-avoiders for years. And home was where Linda's heart was. Stella McCartney has fond memories of those days: "My mum used to have a Mini Cooper," she recalled, in an interview for the *New York Times Magazine* (in which she was the subject of a cover story about her successful career as a fashion designer). "She had it custom-sprayed this metallic hot pink. She had a little microphone put in it, and she would sing to her eight-track. And … she'd always have four dogs in the back. My mum was renowned for collecting us late from school. I'd be on the village lane in Peasmarsh, and all of a sudden—*yeeooww!*—racing around the corner was this pink Mini with Neil Young screaming out."

Then Linda was racing around the world, as Paul launched his first tour since Wings, a decade before. But this wasn't Wings: McCartney's new manager had encouraged him to perform his greatest hits, including a heavy dose of Beatles tunes—almost half of the 32-song set. The formula proved a winning one. Arena crowds everywhere—even in Japan, which forgave and readmitted the man they called Pori Macatnee—were hungry for the great old days; the tour was a smash on four continents. Paul, 47 now, and a little grayer and chubbier, was thrilled.

PAYING A VISIT TO HIS HOMETOWN, in 1989, Paul took a sentimental side trip to see his old school, the Liverpool Institute, which had closed in 1985, the victim of a declining population. He was shocked to see that the grand structure, which he remembered nostalgically, had fallen into complete disrepair, and he resolved to do something about it. Through George Martin, he came up with the idea of creating a Liverpool Institute for the Performing Arts (LIPA) on the site of the original institute and pledged £1 million of his own money to the project, which would finally be completed in 1996.

Liverpool was welcoming back the former prodigal, now its favorite son. In 1991, classical composer Carl Davis, guest conductor of the Royal Liverpool Philharmonic Orchestra and an acquaintance of Paul's, asked him if he'd like to collaborate on a classical piece in honor of the orchestra's 150th anniversary. Boldly enough, since he didn't read or write music, McCartney agreed; the result was *Paul McCartney's Liverpool Oratorio,* which told the story of a charac-

At ease in Los Angeles in 1975, Paul frolics with daughters Stella and Mary. His band is a commercial success, but Paul misses his partnership with John.

ter named Shanty, a kind of alternate-universe version of Paul who grew up in Liverpool and stayed there, becoming part of the city's cycle of life. A recording of the oratorio did very well on the classical-music charts; critical reaction to the piece was mixed, reviewers barely (and sometimes not so barely) suppressing harrumphs of "How dare he?" He dared, and would continue to: further McCartney ventures into classical music, including *Standing Stone* (1997), *Working Classical* (1999), *Ecce Cor Meum* (2006) and *Ocean's Kingdom* (2011), were to follow.

FOR MUCH of 1993, Paul and his band, including Linda, ventured out on the road again, for what he called the New World Tour, playing this time to 1.7 million people on five continents (including Australia/New Zealand) and turning a nice profit. McCartney wouldn't tour again for almost 10 years. It was time to go home.

HOME, IN MORE THAN ONE SENSE: Paul would spend much of 1994 working with George and Ringo on a kind of three-quarters reunion: a Beatles documentary composed of old footage of the band interspersed with contemporary interviews with the three survivors about the great old days. The film, to be called *Anthology,* would also be combined with a companion set of CDs of outtakes, rehearsals and other never-before-heard rarities, including—as a kind of cherry on the sundae—a brand-new Beatles song, "Free As a Bird," assembled from a partial melody John had taped shortly before his death and new material filled in by Paul, George and Ringo.

First, though, there was old business to attend to or, rather, new business based on old: at

PHOTOGRAPH BY HARRY BENSON

at the beginning of the year, Paul inducted John, posthumously, into the Rock and Roll Hall of Fame. (The Beatles had, of course, been inducted as a group in their first year of eligibility, 1988.) "Dear John," Paul's induction speech began, "I remember when we first met, in Woolton, at the village fete." He went on to tell the story of how John had made up lyrics to "Come Go With Me" that hot afternoon, a feat that had never ceased to amaze him.

But then, where Paul was concerned, the same was true of the man himself.

AT THE END OF 1995, the year after Paul and Linda celebrated their 25th wedding anniversary, Linda had a cancerous tumor removed from her left breast. Paul now entered the valley of the shadow of death: it was the same disease that had killed his mother. Over the months that followed, the couple told friends and reporters (for the news was soon out) that Linda was responding to treatment, but she was too unwell to attend the January ceremony in which Paul opened the Liverpool Institute for the Performing Arts, and still too ill the following March to come to Buckingham Palace when Queen Elizabeth dubbed Paul a Knight of the British Empire, making them Sir Paul and Lady McCartney.

In one of Linda's last public appearances before she died, she and Paul, with son James, attend daughter Stella's fashion show in 1997 for the Chloé label.

The shadow deepened. That spring, Paul learned that George Harrison, with whom he'd been at continual artistic odds throughout the making of *Anthology,* had throat cancer that had spread to his lungs.

In October 1997, Linda was able to accompany Paul to Paris to see Stella's first fashion show for the couturier Chloé, and later that fall she attended both the London and New York premieres of her husband's symphonic tone poem *Standing Stone.* The piece was based on a long piece of verse McCartney had written with the same title: the original poem had been inspired by an enigmatic ancient monolith standing in a meadow on their Scottish farm. The lush symphonic piece climaxes with a chorus singing of Paul's great subject, love:

> *Now*
> *with all the time it seemed we had*
> *whatever time I have to spare*
> *will be with you*
> *for ever more.*

But the original poem, which was as stark as the landscape it portrayed, contained this line:

> *She left him to his slab of stone.*

In the early morning hours of April 17, 1998, Linda died in the bedroom of the house she and Paul owned in the Arizona desert. Later that morning, after a private ceremony in Tucson, her body was cremated. It was the first funeral Paul had ever attended.

"IN THAT PERIOD OF TIME when he lost her, we had lots of phone calls," Paul's old Hamburg friend Klaus Voormann recalled recently. "He called us a lot and talked for hours with [me and] my wife. He had to talk to people, and he did. He didn't mind crying. He was very open and very hurt and very emotional. That's the time I was closest to Paul, when he lost his wife. It was terrible."

He went on because he had to go on. His children still needed him, for one thing. In September, he walked his daughter Mary down the aisle at the Church of St. Peter and St. Paul in Peasmarsh, when she married a filmmaker named Alistair Donald. As Linda had been pregnant with Mary when she married Paul, in 1969, Mary was pregnant during the ceremony. The following April, she made her father a grandfather for the first time, when she gave birth to a son, named Arthur.

A few weeks before, at a ceremony in New York City, the Rock and Roll Hall of Fame fulfilled a dying wish of Linda's by inducting Paul, at long last, as a solo artist. Stella McCartney, who attended with her father, wore a white T-shirt that read ABOUT FUCKING TIME!

That May, Paul came further out of mourning to present an award, at a London event celebrating courageous idealists, to a friend of his and Linda's who had worked to promote vegetarianism. Later on in the event, a striking blond stepped onstage to present an honor to a woman who had coped with the loss of two legs and an arm from septicemia. Paul turned to the man sitting next to him—it was Piers Morgan, then the editor of the *Mirror*—and asked, of the blond, "Who's that?"

"That's Heather Mills," Morgan said.

SHE WAS A PIECE OF WORK, to put it mildly. An amputee herself, the 31-year-old had lost her left foot six years earlier, after being struck by a police motorcycle while crossing a London street. Before the accident, Heather Mills had been nobody special—a good-looking, busty young woman from a troubled background who'd run away from a broken home, been arrested for shoplifting and drifted around the edges of the sex industry, working as a barmaid and a photographer's model. After the accident, she became a minor media star, a photogenic, charismatic symbol of courage who crusaded for amputees and land-mine victims and appeared often in the tabloids and on TV. She wrote her autobiography, cleverly titled *Out on a Limb.*

Sir Paul was a sitting duck.

"He was still bereaved, you know, for Linda," Paul's cousin Kate Robbins told TIME. "I mean, he'd been a faithful husband for 30 years; suddenly this blond bombshell comes along saying she needs to support all the charities, do all this charitable [work]—Paul just saw her as a lovely charitable girl."

So much so that he called her to his office and presented her with a check for £150,000—about $230,000—made out to the Heather Mills Health Trust, a charity she advertised in the back of her book. The only problem was, it wasn't a charity: Heather had neglected to register her organization with the Charity Commission. She was funny when it came to details. No matter; soon she and the most famous man in Britain were dating. And very soon, the relationship was more than that.

Paul gets arms in the air in Moscow in 2003, just one stop on a lifelong concert tour.

"I knew she was in love with Paul and he was in love with her, and I thought, 'That's nice,'" Kate Robbins recalled. "But she had a strange way about her. Everything [you] said, she would recall the next time you met and twist it and make it out that you'd said something else. Then you realize that she suffers from this thing of—she's a perpetual liar. It's like an illness ... So we knew there were problems there, because of her past. We knew that she'd lied to Paul about things—and he believed her because he was in love."

New tabloid stories about Heather, suggesting that her past was even seamier than she'd admitted, began to come out. Sir Paul paid no attention. He was rejuvenated. He began recording again, in quick succession releasing a new rock album, *Run Devil Run,* and *Working Classical.* He and Mills traveled to India and the Caribbean by private jet. In Los Angeles, in spring 2001, Paul recorded a new album, *Driving Rain,* in two weeks flat. On the record was a tune called "Heather." That summer, he asked Mills to marry him, and she said yes.

UNLIKE LINDA, HEATHER REVELED in the spotlight. That September, she and Paul went to New York, where she received an award for her charity work. On Sept. 11, the couple was sitting on a commercial plane about to leave John F. Kennedy International for London when the World Trade Center was attacked: from the windows of their plane, Paul and Heather could see the twin towers billowing with smoke, then collapsing.

She persuaded him—Paul was initially reluctant, fearing he'd be seen as trying to promote his new album—to appear at the following month's New York benefit concert in honor of the firefighters and rescue workers of 9/11. Wearing an FDNY T-shirt, he performed a half-dozen songs, including three Beatles numbers, and closed with "Freedom," an anthem he'd written in the wake of the attacks. The audience stomped and cheered as McCartney magic filled Madison Square Garden.

But he could work no magic in November at the bedside of the 58-year-old George Harrison, who lay dying in a Staten Island hospital. Despite their many disagreements, despite George's nearly lifelong feeling that Paul had been condescending and domineering, Paul said that their final moments together were peaceful. "We just sat there stroking hands," he told CNN's Larry King, after Harrison's death on Nov. 29. "And this is a guy, and … you don't stroke hands with guys like that … We just spent a couple of hours, and it was really lovely."

PAUL McCARTNEY AND HEATHER MILLS were married in a splendid ceremony at an Irish castle on June 11, 2002, a week before his 60th birthday. Some 300 guests were present, including Ringo Starr, Mike McCartney (who was his brother's best man, as he'd been at Paul's wedding to Linda), George Martin, Chrissie Hynde and Paul's daughters Mary and Stella. His daughter Heather and son James were conspicuously absent.

After honeymooning that summer, Paul returned to touring, which he'd recommended earlier that year. In McCartney's seventh decade, in the 21st century version of his road show, he was performing 36 numbers per set, 23 of them Beatles songs. In the words of *Daily Mail* reviewer Ray Connolly, Paul and the group were "the best Beatles tribute band in the world."

Paul never seemed to tire of touring, whereas Heather, more a fan of AC/DC than of the Beatles, didn't appear particularly interested in tagging along. Most problematic for her was the feeling that the spotlight was shining on the wrong person, and that in the misdirected glare, both she and her charities were being neglected. "I am married to the most famous person in the world, and that is very unfortunate for me," she told Barbara Walters in a TV interview. "When you become famous at 19, it is sometimes hard to listen to other people's opinions."

"The good side of Heather is incredibly positive and dynamic," Wix Wickens says. "It's that there are no barriers to what you can take on and what you can do. My own view is that she has a damaged family history, and I think that damage comes out in a bad way where she fights everything." Friends and relatives of Paul's noticed her tendency to correct him in public, to prattle on about herself, to change her stories frequently. Paul himself didn't seem to pay it all any mind at first, but as would later become clear, problems with the marriage started cropping up soon after the wedding. There were loud, sometimes violent, arguments, fueled by alcohol or by Heather's unhappiness with Paul's marijuana use. Then came an apparently happy distraction: the birth of their daughter Beatrice Milly, on Oct. 28, 2003.

But the marriage went downhill from there. "We were party to some scenes that should have been more private than they were," Wickens recalls. "I think everybody in the world probably realized that things were not great." Things were worse than that. On April 29, 2006, Paul and

At a castle in Ireland, Paul, 59, kisses fiancée Heather Mills, 34, on the day before their ill-fated marriage.

Heather separated, announcing to the press a month later that the parting was "amicable," and pointing a finger at the media instead of themselves: "[B]oth of us still care about each other very much but have found it increasingly difficult to maintain a normal relationship with the constant intrusion into our private lives."

It was the eve of his 64th birthday—the age he'd imagined, in the song he'd written so long ago, would be all about cozy domesticity.

IN THE END, it all came down to money. In the 2008 divorce proceedings, Sir Paul, whose wealth had been determined by the accounting firm of Ernst & Young to be in the neighborhood of £387 million, or $592 million, was ordered to pay Heather a lump sum of £16.5 million ($25.2 million). She had asked for £125 million.

And the fallout fell on her. "What he went through with that stuff with Heather, it made him even more of a national treasure in this country," Kate Robbins says. "People were just so appalled by what she did."

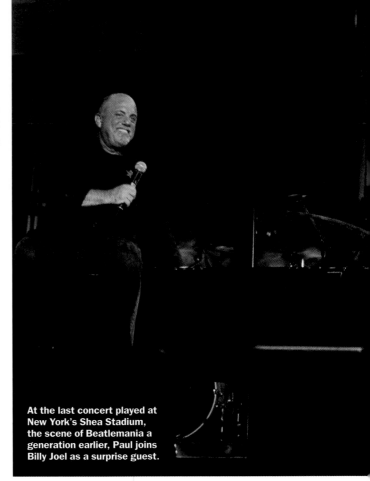

At the last concert played at New York's Shea Stadium, the scene of Beatlemania a generation earlier, Paul joins Billy Joel as a surprise guest.

THAT SUMMER, BILLY JOEL planned a concert to close Shea Stadium, the site of the Beatles' famous 1965 performance, before its demolition to make way for a new arena, Citi Field. He invited McCartney—a friend from New York's Hamptons, where they both owned vacation homes—to play in the show, but Paul couldn't come. "He had a visitation with his kid, which I understood," Joel told TIME. "I said, 'Great, thanks for even considering it.'"

Then scalpers scooped up blocks of tickets for the concert, and Joel, annoyed, scheduled a second and final show. "But I completely forgot about Paul being able to come," he said.

The day of the second show, though, Joel recalled, "I'm driving to Shea Stadium, and I get a call on my cell phone." It was McCartney. "He said, 'Look, I'm leaving London; I don't know if I'll be able to land on time in New York, [but] I'd love to come and play the show.' I thought, 'Oh, my God, that's so cool. But his flight was not going to get in until too late, and he was going to land at JFK, and it would take him too long to get there—there was just no way it's going to happen.'"

"So I kind of forgot about it," Joel said. "But it turned out that the FAA cleared flight space for his plane to land earlier so he could get in. They rushed him through customs. There were all these officials, different security agencies [saying,] 'Just go. Don't worry about customs. Just go. Get in the car.' The police were waiting for him. They got him from JFK airport to Shea Stadium in 11 minutes. Which is humanly impossible. They gave him an escort."

Meanwhile, Joel recalled, "I'm about to wind up the show. I think we had just finished the song

before 'Piano Man,' which is usually the end of the show. I get a tap on my shoulder from my tour manager, Max. He goes, 'The eagle has landed.' I said, 'What?' I turn around, and there's Paul McCartney walking on to the side of the stage, tuning his Hofner bass with a butter knife. I don't know how he got the bass there. He was in his airplane clothes; he's got a tie on, very dapper. He just walks right onstage from flying all the way from England. It must have been five o'clock in the morning to him, and he should have been exhausted. Walked on. He said, 'O.K., Billy, how you doin'?' And BOOM, we did 'I Saw Her Standing There.' We went right into it. In E—the original key. He still sings in those original keys. He's got a freakish voice—he's pushing 70 now, and he's still hitting those notes. I've dropped a bunch of my keys, but he's still up there. He's hitting those Little Richard screams."

After the uproarious applause faded, McCartney yielded the stage to Joel, who played his finale, "Piano Man." But then, Joel said, "we came back. I wanted to do another song with Paul because it's Paul McCartney and we're closing out Shea Stadium. My God, these are the guys who christened the place. I remember when they played at Shea Stadium. It was unheard of. A band is playing in a stadium? [Now] we were going to close the place down, and it was only poetic justice. I said, 'Let It Be.' I just sat on the piano [while McCartney played]. Everybody gave me all this credit for being so magnanimous. Magnanimous? I played a whole show. I'm exhausted. I'm perfectly happy to sit and listen to Paul McCartney play 'Let It Be' to close out Shea Stadium. I'll never forget it."

NOT LONG AFTERWARD, Paul got in his Ford Bronco and, with his new lady friend Nancy Shevell by his side, set out on a cross-country drive, following the path of the legendary Route 66—a drive he'd always wanted to take but, despite all his trips to America, never gotten around to.

He'd first met Shevell, a 47-year-old divorcée, the previous fall, after dating both Rosanna Arquette and Christie Brinkley. Slim, dark-haired, pretty, Shevell was an impressive woman: vice president of a family-owned trucking company and a member of the board of New York's Metropolitan Transit Authority. Like Linda Eastman, she came from a wealthy Jewish family; unlike Linda, Shevell was in midlife, a woman of serious accomplishment, when Paul met her. She had no interest in reaching for a brass ring. It was a new kind of relationship for him, sweet and gradual: they met, they hit it off, they started dating. As they got to know each other, things slowly became more serious.

And now they drove west in the summer of 2008, heading toward a new life.

Credits

FRONT COVER
Mary Ellen Matthews—Corbis Outline

BACK COVER
© Paul Berriff—The Beatles Hidden Gallery

TITLE PAGE
1 © 2003 MPL Communications Ltd./Bill Bernstein

MASTHEAD
3 © 1964 Robert Whitaker

CONTENTS
5 © 2010 MPL Communications Ltd./M.J. Kim

INTRODUCTION
6 © Mike McCartney **8** Michael Ochs Archives—Getty Images **10** © 1970 Paul McCartney/Unidentified Photographer **12** © 2010 MPL Communications Ltd./Photographer: M.J. Kim **17** Andrew Parsons—Polaris Images

A MATCH MADE IN LIVERPOOL
20 © MPL Communications Ltd./McCartney Family **21** "The Day John Met Paul" photo © Geoff Rhind **22** Photographer Leslie Kearney © The Quarrymen **24** (left) © MPL Communications Ltd./McCartney Family; (center) F. Greaves—© Trinity Mirror—Mirrorpix **25** AFP—Getty Images **26** (left) Keystone-France/Gamma-Keystone via Getty Images; (right) Michael Ochs Archives—Getty Images **27** © Mike McCartney **28** (top) Mark and Colleen Hayward—Redferns—Getty Images; (bottom) Christopher Furling—Getty Images **29** Michael Ochs Archives—Getty Images **31** Keystone—Getty Images **32** GAB Archive—Getty Images **33** (bottom and inset top left) Astrid Kirchherr—Courtesy of Vladislav Ginzburg; (inset top right) K & K Ulf Kruger OHG—Redferns—Getty Images **34** Juergen Vollmer—Redferns—Getty Images

MERSEY!
36 Dick Matthews—© Apple Corps Ltd. **39** David Steen—Camera Press—Redux **41** Jane Bown—Camera Press—Redux **42** Tom Hanley—Redferns—Getty Images **43** Popperfoto—Getty Images **45** Chris Ware—Hulton Archive—Getty Images **46** Keystone-France/Gamma-Keystone via Getty Images **48** (left) Paul Berriff—The Beatles Hidden Gallery; (bottom right) Popperfoto—Getty Images **49** (top) Terry O'Neill—Getty Images; (bottom) Jane Bown—Camera Press—Redux **52** (top) Bill Eppridge—Time Life Pictures; (bottom and inset) United Artists—Courtesy Everett Collection Images **53** (top) Bob Gomel—Time Life Pictures; (bottom) Arthur Schatz—Time Life Pictures—Getty **54** John Loengard—Time Life Pictures

GETTING BETTER ALL THE TIME
57 David Montgomery—Getty Images **58** Giorgio Lotti—Mondadori Portfolio via Getty Images **58** Tony Gale—Pictorialpress.com **59** (top) Hulton Archive—Getty Images; Keystone—Getty Images **60** Paul Popper—Popperfoto—Getty Images **61** Robert Whitaker—Getty Images **63** Robert Whitaker—Getty Images **64** (top) NY *Daily News* Archive via Getty Images; (top inset) Tickets Courtesy of www.fab4collectibles.com; (bottom left) Bettmann—Corbis; (bottom right) © Jim Marshall Photography LLC **65** © Bud Gray—PT—Globe Photos **66** Fred W. McDarrah—Getty Images **67** Michael Ochs Archives—Getty Images **69** Robert Whitaker—Getty Images **70** Thomas Picton—Camera Press—Redux **71** Henry Grossman **72** GAB Archive—Redferns—Getty Images **74** John Pratt—Keystone—Hulton Archive—Getty Images **77** (left) Keystone-France—Gamma-Keystone via Getty Images; (right) Photo by Evening Standard—Getty Images **79** (top) Avico Ltd.—Alamy; (bottom left) Popperfoto—Getty Image; (bottom right) Paul Saltzman—Contact Press Images **80** © 1968 Paul McCartney/Photographer: Linda McCartney **81** Andrew Maclear—Hulton Archive—Getty Images **82** Daily Express—Archive Photos—Getty Images

83 (top) © 1970 Paul McCartney/Photographer: Linda McCartney; (bottom) Christie's—Reuters **84** Photo by Bruce McBroom—© Apple Corps Ltd. **86** © Apple Corps Ltd.

WHEN I'M SIXTY-FOUR
88 LIFE Magazine—© Time Inc. **89** © 1969 Paul McCartney/Photographer: Linda McCartney **90** © 1969 Paul McCartney/Photographer: Linda McCartney **91** © 1968 Paul McCartney/Photographer: Linda McCartney **92** (bottom) © Harry Benson 1992; (inset top left) © 1970 Paul McCartney/Photographer: Linda McCartney; (inset top right) © 1979 Paul McCartney/Photographer: Linda McCartney **94** © 1971 Paul McCartney/Photographer: Linda McCartney **97** AFP—Getty Images **99** David Redfern—Redferns—Getty Images **100** "Last photo of Lennon and McCartney" by May Pang (from the book *Instamatic Karma*) **102** Evan Agostini—Liaison—Getty **103** (top) © 1983 MPL Communications Ltd./Photographer: Linda McCartney; (bottom) Popperfoto—Getty Images **105** Photo © Harry Benson **106** Stephane Cardinale—Sygma—Corbis **108** © 2003 MPL Communications Ltd./Photographer: Bill Bernstein **109** Rex USA—BEImages **110** Henry Betrix—Retna Ltd.

THIS PAGE
112 Popperfoto—Getty Images

ENDPAPERS
1962 Höfner Model 500/1 Bass Guitar: photo by Nigel Osbourne/Redferns—Getty Images

All photos © copyright. No reproduction allowed without the express permission of the copyright holders.

Special thanks to Claudia Schmid of MPL Communications Ltd. for her assistance.